BORDEAUX FRANCE

POCKET GUIDE 2025

Explore Vineyards, Historic Charms, Hidden Gems, and Culinary Delights in France's Wine Capital

WanderScript Guides

Table of Contents

INTRODUCTION 9

Chapter 1: Discovering Bordeaux 12

A Brief History of Bordeaux 12

Why Visit Bordeaux in 2025? 14

How to Use This Guide 16

Chapter 2: Key Attractions 19

Chapter 3: Transportation Options 29

Getting to Bordeaux: Flights 29

Getting to Bordeaux: Trains and Buses 31

Public Transport in Bordeaux: Trams, Buses, and V^3 (Bike Rentals) 32

Renting a Car: Driving in Bordeaux and Parking Tips 35

River Cruises on the Garonne 37

Chapter 4: Wine Culture 39

The Wine Capital of the World 39

Famous Wine Regions Around Bordeaux (Medoc, Saint-Emilion, Pomerol) 41

Top Vineyards to Visit 43

Wine Tasting Tours and Workshops 46

Understanding Bordeaux Wine Labels 49

Chapter 5: Historic Sites 53

Bordeaux UNESCO World Heritage Sites 53

The Grosse Cloche 54

Palais Rohan 56

The Roman Amphitheatre (Palais Gallien) 57

Historical Walking Tours 59

Chapter 6: Neighborhoods to Explore 60

Chapter 7: Local Food and Drink 68

Essential Bordeaux Dishes to Try (Canelé, Entrecôte à la
Bordelaise) 68

Best Cafés and Bakeries in Bordeaux 71

Top Restaurants for Fine Dining 74

Markets to Visit (Marché des Capucins, Marché des Grands
Hommes) 77

Local Spirits and Beverages Beyond Wine 79

Chapter 8: Day Trips from Bordeaux 84

Chapter 9: Accommodation Options 98

Luxury Hotels in Bordeaux..98

Mid-Range Hotels:...105

Budget-Friendly Stays:..110

Alternative Accommodations: Apartments, guesthouses, and Airbnb options: 115

Family-Friendly Hotels 119

Chapter 10: Practical Travel Tips..**125**

Getting Around Bordeaux: Trams, Buses, and Bicycles...........125

Currency and Money Matters...127

Language and Communication: Basic French Phrases............129

Mobile Apps for Travelers in Bordeaux.................................131

Understanding French Tipping Etiquette................................132

Chapter 11: Seasonal Events and Festivals............................**134**

Bordeaux Wine Festival (Fête le Vin): 134

The Bordeaux River Festival: 135

Les Epicuriales: Gastronomy Festival:...................................136

The Bordeaux International Independent Film Festival: 137

Christmas Markets and Winter Festivals:................................138

CHAPTER 12: Local Laws and Customs **139**

Essential French Laws for Tourists 139

How to Behave Respectfully in Bordeaux.................. 140

Alcohol, Smoking, and Legal Drinking Ages............... 141

Opening Hours for Shops and Businesses 142

CHAPTER 13: Essentials for Every Traveler 144

What to Pack for a Trip to Bordeaux 144

How to Stay Safe in Bordeaux 145

Traveling with Kids in Bordeaux........................... 147

Accessibility and Mobility in the City 148

CHAPTER 14: 3-day, 5-day, and 7-day itineraries.................150

3-Day Itinerary: Bordeaux Highlights 150

5-Day Itinerary: Explore Bordeaux and Its Wine Regions 153

7-Day Itinerary: Bordeaux, Vineyards, and Nearby Villages. 157

CHAPTER 15: Insider Tips for a WONDERFUL Experience 163

Hidden Gems: Discovering the Lesser-Known Side of Bordeaux

.... 163

Unique Experiences: Cooking Classes, Wine Workshops, and

More 164

Local Markets and Artisanal Boutiques..................... 165

Best Spots for Stunning Views of Bordeaux................................ 165

CHAPTER 16: Traveler Resources and Useful Contacts 167

Tourist Information Centers.. 167

Embassy and Consulate Information.................................... 168

Emergency Numbers and Local Authorities............................. 168

Recommended Travel Agencies and Tour Operators.............. 169

CONCLUSION 171

Bonus: Special Map of Vineyards with Tips for Off-the-Beaten-Path Wineries 172

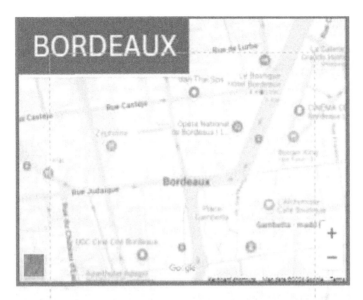

BORDEAUX

SCAN THE QR CODE

- Open your phone's camera.
- Point it at the QR code.
- Wait for the notification.
- Tap the link or prompt.
- Follow the instructions.

INTRODUCTION

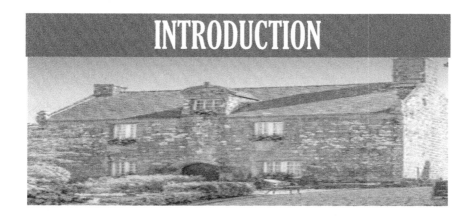

In 2024, I finally had the chance to visit Bordeaux, a city I had heard so much about but never truly understood until I experienced it myself. Though I had been to France before, Bordeaux was a new adventure, and what an unforgettable one it turned out to be.

I felt like I had stepped into a storybook from the moment I arrived. The city has this unique blend of old-world charm and modern elegance. On my first day I started with a walk along the Garonne River. The sun was shining, and the peaceful waters reflected the beautiful buildings that lined the shore. I found myself standing in front of the famous Place de la Bourse and its Miroir d'eau a giant water mirror. It was mesmerizing to watch the reflection of the historic square dance on the water, creating a moment of quiet magic.

Bordeaux isn't just about beautiful sights it's a city that awakens your senses. The food, for example, was a real highlight of my trip. I visited the Marché des Capucins, a local market filled with the freshest produce, meats, and pastries. I indulged in canelés, these little caramelized pastries that Bordeaux is famous for, and enjoyed a glass of local wine. I've always loved French food, but tasting Bordeaux's offerings felt like experiencing food for the first time. Every bite was a connection to the region's traditions.

One of the most memorable parts of my trip was venturing out to the nearby vineyards. The drive through the rolling hills covered in grapevines was breathtaking. I visited a few châteaux and had the opportunity to taste wines directly from where they were made. It wasn't just about drinking wine; it was about understanding the care and passion in each bottle. Sitting in the sun, surrounded by vineyards, sipping on some of the best wine in the world it felt like a dream.

Each day, Bordeaux revealed something new to me. Whether it was the art in the CAPC Museum or the street art scattered throughout the city, I felt like I was constantly discovering something special. In the evenings, I found myself back at the river, watching the city light up as the sun went down. The way the lights reflected on the water created a magical scene I'll never forget.

My experience in Bordeaux was nothing short of wonderful. The city's beauty, the kindness of its people, and the deep connection I felt to its culture made it a trip of a lifetime. I left feeling both inspired and grateful for every moment I spent there.

If you're thinking about visiting Bordeaux, trust me it's a journey worth taking. This city has a way of capturing your heart and leaving you with memories that last long after you've left. And if you want to experience Bordeaux the way I did, get this guidebook. It's filled with tips and insights to help you make the most of your unforgettable adventure.

CHAPTER 1: DISCOVERING BORDEAUX

A Brief History of Bordeaux

Bordeaux is a city that perfectly blends its historical significance with modern vibrancy, making it a top destination for travelers in 2025. Located in southwestern France, Bordeaux's history dates back to its time as a Roman settlement known as Burdigala. Today, it's recognized worldwide for its architectural beauty, wine culture, and riverfront splendor. The city's transformation over the centuries is what makes it so fascinating for visitors.

Bordeaux's charm lies in its well-preserved history, much of which can be seen as you explore its streets. Declared a UNESCO World Heritage site in 2007, the city is one of the largest urban heritage sites in the world, spanning over 1,810 hectares. This means that as you stroll through the heart of Bordeaux, you're walking through centuries of history, from its medieval roots to its 18th-century golden age. The stunning Place de la Bourse, with its classical architecture, stands as a symbol of this era. The square's reflection in the Miroir d'Eau, the world's largest reflecting pool, is a sight that will leave you breathless.

In the 18th century, Bordeaux flourished thanks to the booming wine trade. The city's layout was transformed under the direction of city planners like Tourny, who turned Bordeaux into the elegant and structured city we see today. Wide avenues replaced the medieval walls, and monuments like the Grand Théâtre were built. This era marked the beginning of Bordeaux's recognition as a world leader in wine, a status it continues to hold today.

As you wander the streets of Bordeaux, you'll notice the remnants of its Gallo-Roman past, like the Palais Gallien, an ancient amphitheater that could hold up to 15,000 people. The medieval atmosphere still lingers in areas like the Saint-Pierre district, with its narrow streets and historical landmarks like the Saint-André Cathedral and the Grosse Cloche, one of the oldest belfries in France.

Bordeaux's riverside location played a crucial role in its development, turning it into a bustling port that connected France with the rest of the world. The Port of the Moon, named after the crescent-shaped bend in the Garonne River, is not only visually stunning but historically important as a hub for trade and commerce. Today, you can explore this area on foot or by bike, enjoying the waterfront promenades that offer spectacular views of the city's skyline.

One of Bordeaux's most exciting modern additions is La Cité du Vin, a museum dedicated to the culture of wine. Opened in 2016, this impressive building combines contemporary architecture with interactive exhibitions. Here, you can immerse yourself in the world of wine, learning about its history, tasting local varieties, and enjoying panoramic views of Bordeaux from the museum's terrace.

Bordeaux is not just a city of the past; it's alive with culture, art, and gastronomy. Whether you're visiting the local brasseries or exploring its vibrant street art scene, Bordeaux offers something for every traveler. It's a city that invites you to discover its layers of history while enjoying the modern luxuries that make it a top destination for 2025.

Why Visit Bordeaux in 2025?

Bordeaux is an exceptional destination for 2025, and there are plenty of reasons why it's worth exploring this year. First, its renowned wine culture continues to thrive, making it a paradise for wine lovers. From June 19-22, 2025, the Bordeaux Wine Festival will be held, bringing together wine enthusiasts from around the world. You'll have the chance to enjoy tastings, meet winemakers, and even see the unique tall ships that dock along the quays during this event. Not to mention, Bordeaux's eco-friendly vineyards reflect the city's growing commitment to sustainable tourism.

For foodies, Bordeaux's gastronomic scene is booming. The city is embracing modern culinary trends while still honoring its rich traditions. The blend of new Michelin-starred restaurants with traditional markets like Marché des Capucins ensures a mouthwatering experience. Expect innovative takes on local classics, such as foie gras and canelés, and new wine pairings.

Bordeaux is also stepping into the spotlight for art lovers. The city will host numerous contemporary art exhibitions, immersive experiences, and festivals throughout 2025. The ever-popular Bassins des Lumières offers digital art displays in a stunning setting. With the city's dedication to both modern and traditional art, you'll always find something new to admire

In 2025, Bordeaux's charm goes beyond its wine and food. The Olympic torch relay will pass through the city on May 23, and football fans can enjoy seven matches of the women's and men's football tournament during the Olympic Games in July and August. This will undoubtedly add an extra layer of excitement to the city's already lively atmosphere

Whether you're seeking culture, gastronomy, or just an unforgettable experience, Bordeaux in 2025 is a must-visit.

How to Use This Guide

This guide is designed to be your go-to resource, whether you're a first-time visitor or have been to Bordeaux before. Start by exploring **key attractions** this section highlights must-see landmarks like Place de la Bourse, the Cité du Vin, and Bordeaux's historic city center, a UNESCO World Heritage site. Each attraction includes tips on the best times to visit, ticket information, and what to expect when you get there.

If you're here for Bordeaux's world-famous wine, check out the **wine tours** section. You'll find recommendations for both half-day and full-day tours that take you to the finest vineyards in regions like Médoc and Saint-Émilion. Whether you're a wine novice or an enthusiast, we've included tours that suit every taste and budget.

For **practical travel advice**, you'll find everything you need to know about getting around Bordeaux, from using the city's efficient tram system to where to find the best local food markets. This section also includes up-to-date tips on currency, safety, language, and important phone numbers.

We've created **itineraries** for different types of travelers, so whether you're here for a weekend or a week, there's something for you. These itineraries are flexible and cover a range of interests, from art and history to food and nature.

Finally, don't miss the **day trips** section, perfect for those looking to explore beyond Bordeaux. Whether you want to visit Arcachon Bay for its beaches and seafood or take a trip to the nearby vineyards, we've got you covered with detailed information on transport and things to do.

With this guide, you'll be able to navigate Bordeaux confidently, no matter what kind of traveler you are!

In this travel guide, we've added a fun and interactive feature just for you! In some parts of the book, you'll find **QR codes** that make your journey even more exciting and convenient. All you have to do is scan them with your phone, and voilà you'll instantly be directed to the exact location on your map! Whether it's a cozy hidden vineyard, a top-rated restaurant, or a stunning historical site, these QR codes are like your personal travel assistant, guiding you wherever you want to go.

So, instead of flipping through maps or searching endlessly, just **scan, go, and explore**. It's quick, easy, and lets you enjoy every moment of your adventure with less hassle. Let the QR codes unlock the treasures of Bordeaux at your fingertips. Happy scanning, and enjoy the ride!

CHAPTER 2: KEY ATTRACTIONS

Place de la Bourse and the Water Mirror

Place de la Bourse and the Water Mirror (Miroir d'eau) are two of Bordeaux's most iconic landmarks, seamlessly blending the city's historic charm with modern innovation. Designed in the 18th century by architect Ange-J Jacques Gabriel, **place de la Bourse**  was created to open Bordeaux to the Garonne River, symbolizing the city's wealth and influence during the Age of Enlightenment. Its neoclassical architecture, with intricate mascarons and wrought-iron balconies, creates a stunning backdrop for visitors.

In front of this grand square lies the **Water Mirror**, the world's largest reflecting pool, designed by Michel Corajoud and inaugurated in 2006. This modern masterpiece spans 3,450 square meters and alternates between two mesmerizing effects:

a mirror-like reflection and a mist that envelops the area in a soft fog. Together, these create an enchanting experience, perfect for photos and peaceful walks.

For the best experience, visit during the warmer months (April to October), when the Water Mirror operates fully. The reflection effect is particularly striking at dusk when the golden hues of the sunset reflect off the surface and illuminate the Place de la Bourse. This is also a quieter time, allowing for a more intimate experience, especially in the early morning or late evening.

Visitors can walk through the shallow water and enjoy the playful mist effect, which is especially fun for families. **Photography enthusiasts** will love the opportunity to capture the symmetrical beauty of the square, and sunset shots are a must. Don't forget your tripod for night photos as the Water Mirror is beautifully lit after dark, offering even more dramatic shots of the city's reflection.

For a relaxing meal afterward, the **Saint-Pierre district** is just a short walk away, offering plenty of cozy restaurants and cafés where you can enjoy local cuisine while soaking in the Bordeaux atmosphere.

Bordeaux Cathedral (Saint-André Cathedral)

Saint-André Cathedral is a true gem in the heart of Bordeaux, and a must-see for any traveler in 2025. This UNESCO World Heritage Site, built primarily in the 14th and 15th centuries, stands as a testament to Gothic architecture. Its two towering spires are a striking feature that dominates the skyline. Notably, this is where the famous marriage of Eleanor of Aquitaine to Louis VII took place in 1137, making it a site rich in both religious and political history.

Once you step inside, the high-vaulted ceilings and 19th-century-stained glass windows immediately catch your attention, creating a serene atmosphere that invites reflection. The intricately carved choir stalls are another highlight, as is the grand organ, which still hosts concerts during the Bordeaux International Organ Festival each summer. If you're visiting in August or September, try to catch one of these concerts to experience the cathedral's acoustics at their best.

For those interested in panoramic views, the Pey-Berland bell tower, located next to the cathedral, offers incredible vantage points of the city. The climb is well worth it, especially on a clear day when the views stretch across Bordeaux.

In terms of practical information, the cathedral is open year-round, with winter and summer schedules varying slightly. In summer (June to September), the cathedral is open from **10 AM to 7:30 PM on most days,** while the hours are slightly shorter in winter. **Entry is free,** though donations are appreciated, and guided tours are available in multiple languages.

After your visit, consider stopping by one of the nearby cafés in Place Pey-Berland for a coffee. The square itself is charming, with the Hôtel de Ville (Town Hall) providing an excellent backdrop for photos. Make sure to snap a few pictures of the cathedral's north facade, especially in the late afternoon when the light enhances the details of its stone carvings.

Cité du Vin: The Wine Museum

If you're a wine lover or even just curious about the culture of wine, La Cité du Vin in Bordeaux is a must-visit destination. Opened in 2016, this modern wine museum is dedicated to celebrating the global heritage of wine, and it's an experience that goes beyond traditional exhibitions.

The museum is an architectural masterpiece, designed to resemble the swirl of wine in a glass. Inside, you'll find over 20 themed spaces that cover everything from the history of wine to the science of winemaking. Interactive exhibits use multimedia, including 3D displays and immersive storytelling, making the museum accessible and engaging for visitors of all ages. One of the most unique features is the immersive visual art installation—an extraordinary fusion of wine and culture.

Practical information for 2024 travelers: La Cité du Vin is open from 10 a.m. to 7 p.m. from March to November, with slightly reduced hours during the winter months. It's best to plan a 3-4 hour visit to fully experience the exhibitions, the panoramic views from the 8th-floor Belvedere, and of course, the wine tasting included with your ticket. Be sure to buy tickets in advance, especially during the busy months of May through August, to avoid long queues. Tickets are €22 for adults, and the price includes a wine tasting from a global selection.

One tip for photography enthusiasts: the panoramic views of Bordeaux from the top floor are unbeatable, especially during sunset. After your visit, you can explore nearby attractions like the Les Halles de Bacalan food market or enjoy a meal at Le 7 Restaurant, which offers 360-degree views of the city while you dine on local delicacies.

Whether you're deepening your knowledge of Bordeaux's wine culture or simply enjoying a glass with a view, La Cité du Vin is an unforgettable stop on your journey through this historic wine region

Pey-Berland Tower

Pey-Berland Tower is a must-see for anyone visiting Bordeaux. Built in the 15th century, this Gothic-style belfry was constructed separately from the nearby Saint-André Cathedral due to concerns that the weight of the bells could damage the cathedral's structure. Today, it stands as an iconic part of Bordeaux's skyline, offering both a historical journey and some of the best panoramic views in the city.

Climbing Pey-Berland Tower is an adventure in itself. To reach the top, you'll need to conquer 231 narrow, spiral steps. While the climb might seem daunting, the reward at the top is worth every step. From the summit, you'll have a breathtaking 360-degree view of Bordeaux, including the cathedral, the Garonne River, and the rolling rooftops of the city. For the best experience, plan your visit early in the morning or late afternoon. These times offer fewer crowds and the soft, golden light makes for stunning photographs.

In 2024, the tower is open daily from 10:00 AM to 6:00 PM, though it's wise to check for any updates on hours due to possible renovations or special events. The tower is not fully accessible to those with mobility issues due to the steep staircase, so plan accordingly if you have concerns.

One tip: after your climb, take a break at one of the nearby cafés, like Café Français, where you can enjoy a coffee with a view of the cathedral. And if you're a photography enthusiast, the light at sunset creates the perfect backdrop for capturing Bordeaux's beauty from the top.

Whether you're a history buff or just looking for incredible views, Pey-Berland Tower offers an experience you won't want to miss during your time in Bordeaux.

Grand Théâtre de Bordeaux

The **Grand Théâtre de Bordeaux**, an 18th-century gem, is one of the most iconic landmarks in the city and a must-see for any visitor. Designed by the renowned architect **Victor Louis** and completed in 1780, the theater is a stunning example of neoclassical architecture. Its magnificent façade is adorned with twelve Corinthian columns, and statues representing the muses and goddesses greet visitors at the entrance, setting the stage for the artistic wonders inside.

Upon entering, you are greeted by the grand stone staircase, leading you to a lavish interior decorated in royal hues of blue, white, and gold. The horseshoe-shaped auditorium, crowned by a sparkling crystal chandelier, has hosted countless performances throughout history and is known for its impeccable acoustics. Today, the Grand Théâtre remains the home of the **Bordeaux National Opera** and continues to host operas, ballets, and classical concerts.

For those eager to explore beyond the performances, **guided tours** are available on Wednesdays and Saturdays, offering a deeper look into the theater's rich history and architecture. These tours typically run at 2:00 PM, 3:30 PM, and 5:00 PM, but it's best to check the theater's official website for updated schedules and ticket availability.

If you're planning to catch a performance, the theater's calendar is packed with spectacular shows throughout the year. Be sure to book your tickets well in advance, as the most popular performances tend to sell out quickly. Visitors with disabilities will find accessible seating options, and it's a good idea to contact the theater ahead of time for any special accommodations.

After your visit, enjoy a meal at one of the many nearby restaurants at **Place de la Comédie**, or simply admire the beauty of this historic square while capturing stunning photographs of the theater's impressive exterior

The Garonne River Walk

The Garonne River Walk is one of the best ways to experience the beauty of Bordeaux while enjoying the city's rich history and modern flair. This scenic path runs alongside the Garonne River, offering stunning views of both the water and Bordeaux's magnificent architecture. Originally an important trade route, the river has shaped the city's growth, and today, it remains a vital part of Bordeaux's culture and lifestyle.

As you walk along the river, you'll notice the blend of old and new historic stone bridges like the Pont de Pierre, with its arches gracefully spanning the Garonne and contemporary architecture like the sleek Cité du Vin wine museum. The stretch near the Pont de Pierre is perfect for a peaceful stroll or bike ride. If you're a fan of photography, this spot is ideal for capturing the city's skyline reflected in the water, especially during sunset when the golden light creates a magical atmosphere.

For a relaxing break, stop at one of the many cafes or bars nearby, such as La Cité du Vin's rooftop bar, which offers panoramic views of the river and the city. It's a perfect place to unwind with a glass of Bordeaux wine. If you're looking for something lighter, head to the cafés around the Place des Quinconces, just a short walk from the riverfront.

The Garonne River Walk is accessible year-round, but it's best enjoyed during the spring and fall when the weather is mild. Early morning or late afternoon is the perfect time for a visit, avoiding the midday heat while enjoying the quiet ambiance. With easy access for pedestrians and cyclists, it's a must-see for anyone visiting Bordeaux in 2025.

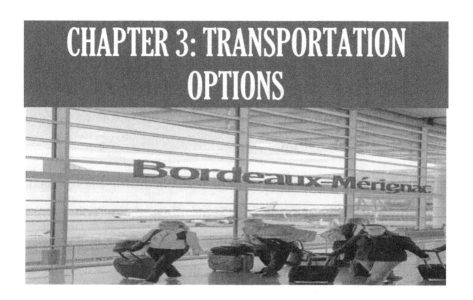

CHAPTER 3: TRANSPORTATION OPTIONS

Getting to Bordeaux: Flights

Flying into Bordeaux in 2025 is a convenient and enjoyable experience, especially with Bordeaux–Mérignac Airport (BOD) serving as a major gateway for international and domestic travelers. Located just 12 kilometers (7.5 miles) west of Bordeaux, the airport is well-connected to cities across Europe and beyond.

Several major airlines offer direct flights to Bordeaux. For international travelers, popular routes include Air France from Paris, KLM from Amsterdam, Iberia from Madrid, and British Airways from London. Domestic flights are also frequent, with easyJet and Ryanair being top choices for affordable flights within Europe. From North America, while there are no direct flights to Bordeaux, connecting flights via Paris or London are the most common options. Expect flight times from New York or other major U.S. cities to take around 11 hours with a layover, and average round-trip prices ranging from $700 to $1,500 depending on the season.

The best time to book flights to Bordeaux is during the off-peak season, which includes the fall (September to November) and early spring (March to May). Prices tend to be lower, and the city is less crowded. Booking 3-6 months in advance is recommended for the best deals.

Once you arrive at Bordeaux–Mérignac Airport, reaching the city center is easy. The 30-minute express bus service, "Liane 1," operates frequently and costs around €2. Alternatively, you can opt for taxis, which cost approximately €30–€40 depending on traffic. Car rentals are also available at the airport if you plan to explore the nearby vineyards or countryside.

The airport offers modern amenities, including duty-free shopping, dining options, and currency exchange services. Arriving travelers should expect a smooth process through customs, but it's always a good idea to check for any travel restrictions or requirements beforehand.

Getting to Bordeaux: Trains and Buses

Traveling to Bordeaux by train or bus is convenient, fast, and eco-friendly, making it a great choice for tourists in 2025. For those arriving from Paris, **the TGV (high-speed train)** is the best option. It runs several times daily from Paris Montparnasse to Bordeaux Saint-Jean, with travel times as short as 2 hours and 4 minutes. Ticket prices can be very affordable if booked in advance, starting around **€20** for standard class, while first-class tickets offer added comfort with larger seats and **Wi-Fi access.** If you prefer a more budget-friendly option, **OUIGO trains** also offer low-cost journeys from Paris to Bordeaux, but with fewer amenities.

Regional trains, such as the **TER services,** are perfect for exploring the Nouvelle-Aquitaine region around Bordeaux. These trains don't require reserved seats, so you can hop on without booking in advance, although it's always best to check schedules. Keep in mind that TER trains operate on a fixed price, making them less expensive but still very efficient.

If you prefer to travel by bus, **FlixBus** provides regular services from major French cities to Bordeaux. For instance, buses from Paris to Bordeaux take about 7 hours and cost between **€20 and €50,** depending on how early you book. Buses are equipped with Wi-Fi, power outlets, and comfortable seats, making the journey enjoyable even over longer distances. BlaBlaCar Bus is another option, offering competitive prices and comfortable seating.

Both Bordeaux Saint-Jean train station and bus terminals are easy to navigate, with clear signage in French and English. Arrive at the station 30-60 minutes before departure to find your platform or gate. For a more eco-conscious journey, both trains and buses offer lower carbon footprints compared to flying, making them ideal for eco-friendly travelers.

Public Transport in Bordeaux: Trams, Buses, and V³ (Bike Rentals)

In Bordeaux, cruising the city with ease is made possible by its efficient public transport system. Whether you're exploring the bustling streets or heading to vineyards outside the city, the options of trams, buses, and V^3 bike rentals make it simple for tourists to get around.

Trams in Bordeaux

Bordeaux's tram system is modern, reliable, and easy to use. There are four main lines A, B, C, and D that run across the city, connecting key areas and attractions like the Place de la Bourse, the Cité du Vin, and Saint-Jean Train Station. Trams operate *from 5:00 AM to midnight on weekdays, with extended hours* on weekends, making it convenient for day trips or late-night exploration. During peak hours, trams arrive every 4 to 7 minutes, while at night, you can expect them every 8 to 15 minutes.

For tourists, the best ticket option is the **CityPass** which costs around €34 for 24 hours, €44 for 48 hours, or €50 for 72 hours. This pass includes unlimited access to the tram, buses, and even riverboats (Bat^3). It also provides free entry to various museums and guided tours, giving you more value during your stay.

When using trams, always validate your ticket at the machines available on the platform. Failure to do so can result in a hefty fine of €122, so make sure your pass is correctly validated before each trip. Tickets can be bought from vending machines at tram stops, or through mobile apps for easy and cashless transactions

Buses in Bordeaux

Bordeaux's bus network is extensive, with over 70 lines serving the metropolitan area. These buses are perfect for reaching places that the trams don't cover. Night buses also operate on specific routes, allowing you to move around the city safely after dark.

For tourists, bus tickets are integrated with the tram system, so a single ticket can be used on both forms of transport. If you're planning multiple trips in one day, a **7-day pass for €14.20** might be the best option, giving you unlimited rides on both buses and trams. As with the trams, remember to signal to the driver if you wish to board a bus, and press the red button inside to request your stop

V^3 (Bike Rentals)

For those looking for a more active and scenic way to explore, Bordeaux's **V^3 (VCub)** bike rental system is perfect. With over 2,000 bikes available at 186 stations across the city, you can easily pick up and drop off bikes at major locations. The system operates 24/7, and you can rent a bike for just **€1.70 per day** or **€7.70 for a week**. The first 30 minutes of each ride are free, and after that, a small fee of **€2 per hour** applies, which is automatically charged to the card you used to rent the bike.

One great feature of the V^3 system is its user-friendly mobile app, which allows you to check bike availability and find docking stations in real-time. Some of the best cycling routes include a ride along the Garonne River or through the lush Parc Bordelais, giving you a perfect mix of nature and urban views

Practical Tips

Download the **TBM** or **V³ mobile apps** to plan your trips efficiently and make sure you have access to real-time updates on tram and bus schedules, as well as bike availability.

Both apps allow you to buy tickets directly from your phone, making it hassle-free. Credit cards are widely accepted across the transport system, so you don't need to worry about carrying cash.

With these options, Bordeaux offers a smooth and enjoyable transportation experience. Whether you're exploring by tram, bus, or bike, you'll find that the city's public transport is designed to help you get the most out of your visit.

Renting a Car: Driving in Bordeaux and Parking Tips

Renting a car in Bordeaux can be a great option, especially if you plan to tour the surrounding wine regions, but it's important to know a few things before hitting the road.

Car Rental Providers & Costs: Major car rental companies like Hertz, Sixt, Enterprise, and Europcar are available at Bordeaux Airport and in the city center. Prices for car rentals generally start around €35 per day for small, manual cars, with automatic options costing more. Booking in advance will help you secure better rates, particularly during the high season.

Documents Needed: To rent a car, you must be at least 21 years old, though some companies require you to be 25. You'll need a valid driver's license, held for at least one year, and a credit card for the security deposit. For non-EU residents, an International Driver's Permit is recommended but not mandatory.

Insurance coverage is also essential, and you can either opt for the rental company's policy or ensure your travel insurance covers car rentals.

Driving in Bordeaux: Bordeaux's streets can be narrow, and the city has many pedestrian areas. Opt for a smaller car for easier navigation and parking. Traffic rules are strict always wear seat belts, and note that using mobile phones while driving is prohibited. Bordeaux's public transportation is excellent, so consider whether you truly need a car for in-city travel.

Parking Tips: Parking can be tricky and expensive. Street parking in the city center costs around €2.50 per hour, with free hours in the evenings and on Sundays. Parking garages, such as those run by Metpark, offer more secure options at about €20 per day. The EasyPark app is useful for paying parking fees via your smartphone. If you're visiting the city's outskirts or vineyards, parking is generally easier and more available.

For an easy and stress-free experience, plan ahead, understand parking rules and evaluate if renting a car fits your itinerary

River Cruises on the Garonne

One of the best ways to tour Bordeaux's beauty and history is through a river cruise on the Garonne. Whether you're interested in sightseeing or indulging in local wines, these cruises offer something for everyone.

A popular option is the 90-minute guided sightseeing cruise, which gives you stunning views of iconic landmarks like the **Place de la Bourse, Pont de Pierre, and the Port of the Moon, a UNESCO World Heritage site**. As you sail, a knowledgeable guide shares fascinating insights into the city's Roman history, its golden age of trade, and modern culture. The cruise also passes by the **stunning Cité du Vin, Bordeaux's celebrated wine museum.**

If you're a wine lover, you can't miss the wine-tasting cruises. These special tours combine scenic river views with tastings of local Bordeaux wines. One such tour, departing from La Cité du Vin, includes tastings of two prestigious wines along with expert commentary on Bordeaux's rich winemaking traditions.

Onboard, you'll be served a glass of wine accompanied by a delicious canelé, a local pastry.

For booking, it's recommended to make reservations early, especially during the busy summer months. Prices start around **€19 for a basic sightseeing cruise and €28 for wine-tasting cruises.** The cruises are available year-round, though the best time to go is in late spring or early fall when the weather is pleasant and the riverbanks are lush with greenery. Cruises usually depart from the **Ponton d'Honneur,** and you'll want to arrive at least 30 minutes early to secure your spot.

Whether you're looking to relax or learn more about Bordeaux's rich heritage, a river cruise offers a memorable experience. Combine it with a walking tour of Bordeaux's historic districts to round out your adventure!

CHAPTER 4: WINE CULTURE

The Wine Capital of the World

Bordeaux:

Bordeaux is truly a dream destination for wine lovers. Known globally as the "Wine Capital of the World," Bordeaux's connection to wine runs deep. The city is surrounded by over 7,000 châteaux spread across 300,000 acres of vineyards, producing some of the world's most famous wines, including renowned reds like Merlot and Cabernet Sauvignon. This legacy of winemaking spans over 2,000 years, dating back to Roman times. It's a tradition passed down through generations, with each winemaker building on the craftsmanship of their ancestors to produce wines that are both elegant and complex.

Bordeaux's influence on global wine culture cannot be overstated. The region is home to some of the most prestigious wine appellations, including Médoc, Saint-Émilion, and Pomerol, which have become benchmarks for quality and tradition in the wine world. For many, a visit to Bordeaux is like stepping into a living history of wine. Whether you're touring the grand châteaux, like Château Margaux or Château Lafite Rothschild, or learning about winemaking techniques, the experience is nothing short of extraordinary.

A visit to Bordeaux isn't just about drinking wine; it's about understanding the story behind each bottle. La Cité du Vin, a wine museum in the city, offers a multi-sensory journey through wine history and culture, allowing visitors to immerse themselves in the rich heritage of this iconic region. From interactive exhibits to wine-tasting workshops, this modern institution highlights the significance of Bordeaux wines on a global scale.

For any wine enthusiast or curious traveler, Bordeaux offers an unforgettable experience combining the beauty of the vineyards with the sophistication of its wines.

Famous Wine Regions Around Bordeaux (Medoc, Saint-Emilion, Pomerol)

When you visit Bordeaux, you're stepping into a world where wine is not just a drink, but a way of life. Some of the most famous wine regions in the world surround the city, each offering something unique for travelers. Among these regions, Médoc, Saint-Emilion, and Pomerol stand out, both for their breathtaking landscapes and for the exceptional wines they produce.

Médoc

Located on the Left Bank of the Gironde River, Médoc is known for its powerful red wines, particularly those made with Cabernet Sauvignon. The region's terroir—composed of gravel and clay soils—helps the vines dig deep for water, which leads to low-yield, high-quality grapes. Médoc is famous for its "Route des Châteaux," a scenic road lined with stunning vineyards and prestigious estates like Château Margaux and Château Lafite-Rothschild. A tour of the region takes you through iconic appellations such as Pauillac, Saint-Julien, and Margaux. The wines here are structured and tannic, built to age gracefully, with flavors of dark fruit, tobacco, and spice. If you love bold wines with depth, Médoc is the place to visit

Saint-Emilion

On the Right Bank of the Dordogne River, Saint-Emilion offers a completely different experience. The region's Merlot-dominant wines are softer and more approachable than the robust Médoc reds. Walking through the medieval village of Saint-Emilion feels like stepping back in time. The narrow streets are lined with charming cafés, and the village is a UNESCO World Heritage site thanks to its long history. Saint-Emilion is known for its limestone-rich soils, which contribute to the unique elegance of its wines. Famous wineries like Château Angélus and Château Cheval Blanc produce some of the best Merlot-based wines in the world. The wines from this region are known for their smooth, velvety textures, and aromas of red berries and plums. Whether you're a novice or a seasoned wine lover, tasting the wines here while soaking in the town's history is an unforgettable experience

Pomerol

Just a short drive from Saint-Emilion, Pomerol is smaller but no less significant. This region is famous for producing some of the most luxurious and expensive wines in the world, particularly from Château Pétrus. Unlike the larger estates of Médoc and Saint-Emilion, Pomerol's wineries are often family-run, adding a personal touch to your visit. The clay soils here are perfect for

Merlot, which thrives in this area, producing wines that are rich, full-bodied, and layered with notes of truffle, black cherries, and violets. Pomerol wines are opulent yet refined, offering a different expression of Bordeaux's famed Merlot grape

Each of these regions offers its slice of Bordeaux wine culture, making them essential stops for anyone visiting the area. Whether you prefer the bold, structured wines of Médoc, the elegant charm of Saint-Emilion, or the luxurious richness of Pomerol, you'll find something to fall in love with in Bordeaux.

Top Vineyards to Visit

When visiting Bordeaux in 2024, you'll find that its vineyards offer an unforgettable experience. Whether you're a wine enthusiast or just curious to explore, the region has something unique to offer. Here are some of the top vineyards you should consider adding to your itinerary.

Château Margaux:

Located in the Médoc region on Bordeaux's Left Bank, Château Margaux is one of the most famous wine estates in the world. Known for its Premier Grand Cru Classé (First Growth) status, this estate offers an immersive experience into the history and winemaking process.

Visitors can explore the breathtaking architecture, tour the historic cellars, and enjoy tastings of their exquisite red wines. The tours here allow you to witness the precision and care that goes into producing one of the world's most iconic wines. Booking in advance is highly recommended, as this château is very popular among wine lovers.

Château Latour:

Another Médoc treasure, Château Latour is synonymous with prestige. Its wines are celebrated for their structure, elegance, and aging potential. Château Latour offers private tours where you can dive deep into the estate's rich history and winemaking processes. You'll have the chance to sample vintages known for their complex flavors of blackcurrant and cedar. It's a perfect stop for anyone wanting to experience Bordeaux's wine heritage up close.

Château Lafite Rothschild:

Situated in Pauillac, Château Lafite Rothschild is another must-visit for lovers of Cabernet Sauvignon-based wines. The estate's rich history and attention to detail have made it one of the most sought-after wine destinations in Bordeaux. A visit here provides a tour of the ancient cellars and an opportunity to taste the fine, tannic wines that have made Château Lafite Rothschild a household name among connoisseurs.

Château Haut-Brion:

For those looking to explore beyond the Médoc, Château Haut-Brion, located in Pessac-Léognan, offers a unique experience. As the only estate from outside the Médoc included in the 1855 classification, Château Haut-Brion produces both exceptional red and white wines. Visitors can enjoy a guided tour of the vineyards and cellars, followed by a tasting session where they will discover the deep complexity of this estate's wines.

Château Cheval Blanc:

On the Right Bank, in the heart of Saint-Émilion, Château Cheval Blanc stands out for its world-renowned Merlot and Cabernet Franc blends. This château provides a fascinating look at modern winemaking techniques in a region steeped in tradition. Guests can explore the sleek, contemporary winery and enjoy a personalized wine tasting. It's an excellent stop if you're looking to compare the styles between Left and Right Bank wines.

Château d'Yquem:

If sweet wines are your preference, Château d'Yquem in the Sauternes appellation is not to be missed. This estate produces some of the world's finest dessert wines, made from grapes affected by noble rot, which concentrates the sweetness and flavor. A tour here allows you to see the meticulous process involved in creating their legendary wines, followed by a tasting that is sure to delight your palate.

These vineyards not only showcase the best of Bordeaux's wine culture but also offer immersive experiences that go beyond tastings. Whether you're exploring ancient cellars, learning about winemaking techniques, or simply enjoying the stunning vineyard views, each visit promises to leave you with lasting memories. Make sure to book your tours early, as these famous estates are often fully booked during peak seasons.

Wine Tasting Tours and Workshops

When it comes to wine culture in Bordeaux, there's truly no better way to immerse yourself in the region than through wine-tasting tours and workshops. Bordeaux is world-renowned for its wines, and whether you're a beginner or a seasoned connoisseur, there are experiences to match your interests and level of expertise.

Large-Scale Wine Tours For a classic introduction to Bordeaux's vineyards, a full-day tour is a great way to start. Popular options include visits to the Médoc and Saint-Émilion wine regions. These tours typically take you to several wineries, or "châteaux," and give you a comprehensive look at wine production, from grape to bottle.

For example, a full-day tour from Bordeaux to Saint-Émilion offers wine tastings at multiple estates and a guided walking tour of the historic village, which is a UNESCO World Heritage site. You'll sample Grand Cru wines while exploring picturesque vineyards, and lunch is often included, giving you a chance to relax while enjoying the local fare. This type of tour is great for those who want to cover a lot in one day and enjoy tasting wines at some of the most prestigious estates in the region.

Alternatively, a tour through the Médoc region will take you to renowned wineries such as Château Margaux and Château Palmer. These visits usually include tastings of both red and white wines and provide insight into the history of the estates.

Intimate Wine Workshops For those looking to dive deeper into the intricacies of wine tasting, smaller, more focused workshops are the way to go. Many vineyards offer private or small-group workshops where you can learn directly from the experts. One popular option is a "make your own cuvée" workshop, where you get hands-on experience blending different grape varieties to create your own custom wine. This workshop is ideal for anyone who wants a deeper, more interactive experience, as you get to bottle and label your creation to take home.

Another great option is the Bordeaux Wine Fundamentals workshop, which focuses on developing your palate. These sessions usually include a tasting of several different wines paired with local cheeses or charcuterie, making it a perfect introduction for beginners who want to learn the basics of wine appreciation.

Unique Experiences For a more adventurous wine tasting experience, consider an electric bike tour through the vineyards of Saint-Émilion. This eco-friendly option allows you to cycle through the countryside at a leisurely pace, stopping at wineries for tastings along the way. It's a great way to combine some light exercise with wine tasting while taking in the beautiful landscape of Bordeaux's vineyards.

Lastly, for something truly unique, you can even take a wine-tasting cruise along the Garonne River. These cruises provide stunning views of the city's historic architecture while you sip on Bordeaux's finest wines and enjoy local delicacies like canelés.

Understanding Bordeaux Wine Labels

When visiting Bordeaux, understanding the wine labels can enhance your experience, helping you pick the perfect bottle to suit your taste. Bordeaux wine labels may seem complex at first, but they follow a structured system that reflects the region's commitment to quality and tradition. Here's what you need to know.

Appellation d'Origine Contrôlée (AOC)

The first thing you'll notice on a Bordeaux wine label is the appellation, or AOC (Appellation d'Origine Contrôlée). This tells you where the grapes were grown and ensures that the wine follows specific regulations for quality. There are several AOCs in Bordeaux, such as Médoc, Pauillac, and Saint-Émilion. Each of these regions produces wines with unique characteristics, heavily influenced by their terroir (the combination of soil, climate, and vineyard practices).

If you see "Bordeaux AOC" on the label, this generally indicates a broad regional wine, whereas more specific appellations like "Pauillac" or "Margaux" signal wines with more distinct characteristics, often associated with a higher level of prestige and complexity. Understanding the AOC will help you gauge the style of the wine you're choosing.

Vintage

Another important detail on Bordeaux wine labels is the vintage, or the year the grapes were harvested. In Bordeaux, the weather varies greatly from year to year, which can have a significant impact on the quality of the wine. Some years, like 2009 and 2010, are considered exceptional, while others may not be as favorable. As a general rule, wines from great vintages will be more expensive, but they also offer a richer tasting experience.

Cru Classifications

Bordeaux is known for its "Cru" system, which classifies vineyards based on their historical reputation and quality. There are several levels of classification, and each tells you something about the wine's pedigree:

1. **Grand Cru Classé**: Established in 1855, this classification applies mostly to the Médoc and Sauternes regions. There are five levels (called growths), with First Growths being the most prestigious. Wineries like Château Margaux and Château Latour belong to this top tier.

2. **Premier Grand Cru Classé**: This is a higher classification seen in Saint-Émilion. It's divided into two categories: Premier Grand Cru Classé A (the absolute top) and B (still exceptional but slightly lower). These wines are reclassified every decade, so they maintain high standards.

3. **Cru Bourgeois**: A more recent classification from the Médoc region, the Cru Bourgeois is meant for high-quality wines that don't fall into the 1855 classification. These wines offer excellent value for money.

4. **Bordeaux Supérieur**: This indicates wines with stricter production standards than regular Bordeaux AOC wines. These wines often come from older vines and have a slightly higher alcohol content, resulting in a richer flavor profile.

Tips for Tourists

When shopping for Bordeaux wines, always check for the **AOC** to understand the wine's origin, the **vintage** to gauge quality, and any **Cru classification** to assess prestige. If you're unsure, the classification is a helpful guide. Premier Cru and Grand Cru wines are great for special occasions, while Bordeaux Supérieur and Cru Bourgeois are excellent for everyday drinking.

Remember, Bordeaux wines are known for their aging potential. If you're looking to enjoy a bottle soon, opt for a wine that's already a few years old, or ask a local wine merchant for recommendations based on your preferences.

CHAPTER 5: HISTORIC SITES

Bordeaux UNESCO World Heritage Sites

Bordeaux's historic center, known as the "Port of the Moon," was designated a UNESCO World Heritage Site in 2007, thanks to its remarkable urban planning and neoclassical architecture. This area covers 1,810 hectares and includes over 350 historical monuments, making it one of the largest World Heritage urban areas in the world.

The city's layout, shaped like a crescent along the Garonne River, has remained largely unchanged since the 18th century, when it was developed as a center of trade and culture. Bordeaux's significance lies in its role as a cultural and commercial hub, connecting France with Britain and other parts of Europe for over two millennia.

A must-visit site is the Place de la Bourse, which is famous for its elegant neoclassical design and stunning water mirror, the

Miroir d'Eau. This modern feature beautifully reflects the grand customs buildings behind it, creating an iconic view, especially during sunrise and sunset.

Another key highlight is the Bordeaux Cathedral, a Gothic masterpiece that has witnessed royal weddings and significant events in French history. Nearby, the Pey Berland Tower offers visitors a breathtaking panoramic view of the city, but be prepared for the climb 229 steps lead to the top!

For a deeper Bordeaux's historical and architectural splendor, don't miss the Palais Rohan, now serving as the city's town hall. This former archbishop's palace embodies Bordeaux's rich blend of political and religious history.

Visiting Bordeaux in 2025 is an opportunity to experience a city that harmoniously merges its Enlightenment heritage with modern innovations. Whether you're exploring its magnificent buildings or simply enjoying a wine tasting, Bordeaux's UNESCO-listed sites offer a journey through time you won't want to miss.

The Grosse Cloche

The Grosse Cloche, one of the most iconic landmarks in Bordeaux, offers a fascinating glimpse into the city's medieval past. Standing proudly in the heart of Bordeaux, this bell tower was originally part of the city's defensive walls and has witnessed centuries of history. Built-in the 13th century as part of the Porte Saint-Éloi, it was later fitted with the famous bell that gives it its name. The bell, cast in 1775, weighs over 7,750 kilos and rings only on special occasions, such as Bastille Day and VE Day, and on the first Sunday of each month at noon.

The Grosse Cloche was not just a bell tower; it also served as a prison during the Middle Ages. The thick, bolted doors of the dungeon held young offenders, and legends still linger about the eerie atmosphere inside. Visitors can explore these dungeons, where guides recount stories of those who violated curfews or public order.

Architecturally, the Grosse Cloche is a blend of Gothic and medieval styles, crowned by two turrets topped with pointed, witch-hat roofs. The bell itself, named "Armande-Louise," is not only a striking feature but a symbol of the city's resilience and pride. The inscriptions on the bell reveal its purpose: to ring out for both joyous occasions and mournful events.

As a tourist, the Grosse Cloche offers more than just a photo opportunity. You can immerse yourself in Bordeaux's history while taking in the beauty of the surrounding Rue Saint-James, a lively street with boutiques and cafes. The best time to visit is in spring or fall when the weather is pleasant and crowds are thinner.

If you're planning a trip to Bordeaux, make sure to tour the Grosse Cloche it's a step back in time and an essential part of the city's cultural fabric.

Palais Rohan

The **Palais Rohan**, known today as Bordeaux City Hall, is one of the city's most important landmarks. Built between 1771 and 1784, the palace originally served as the residence for the Archbishop of Bordeaux, **Ferdinand Maximilien Mériadec de Rohan**, and was later transformed into the city hall in 1837. Its neoclassical architecture reflects a mix of elegance and historical significance, making it a must-visit for any traveler interested in Bordeaux's rich heritage.

As you tour the **Palais Rohan**, you'll be captivated by its grand **façade**, featuring intricate stonework and large windows that give the building its majestic presence. Inside, you'll find even more treasures: the beautifully preserved **wood-carved interiors**, trompe-l'œil paintings by **Pierre Lacour**, and a grand staircase considered a masterpiece of stone masonry from the period.

Tours of the **Palais Rohan** are offered twice a week, but they are only available in French, so be prepared for that if you decide to join one. Booking a tour through the Bordeaux Tourist Office is essential, as the palace can only be accessed with a guided visit. These tours not only allow you to appreciate the architecture but also give insight into the building's long and colorful history. The tours often highlight key moments, such as its transformation into a royal residence under **Napoleon** and its role in Bordeaux's modern governance.

For a more immersive experience, consider purchasing the **Bordeaux City Pass**, which offers access to various historical sites, including the Palais Rohan, along with perks like public transportation don't miss out on this architectural gem. Its grandeur, history, and cultural significance are sure to leave a lasting impression.

The Roman Amphitheatre (Palais Gallien)

The Palais Gallien is one of Bordeaux's most remarkable remnants of Roman history. Built in the 2nd century AD during the height of the Roman Empire, this amphitheater was once a grand venue for gladiatorial contests, animal hunts, and public spectacles. With a seating capacity of around 15,000 people, it stood as a symbol of Roman power and culture in the ancient city of Burdigala, now Bordeaux.

Today, what remains of the Palais Gallien offers visitors a fascinating glimpse into the past. Though much of the original structure has been lost over time some stones were even repurposed for other buildings in the Middle Ages the surviving ruins still tell a powerful story. As you walk among the ancient arches and walls, you can almost hear the echoes of the crowds and imagine the grand scale of the events that once took place here.

Located just a short distance from Bordeaux's city center, this site is easy to access and offers a tranquil escape from the bustling streets. The amphitheater's monumental gateway, which still stands, gives you a sense of the sheer size of the original structure. Nearby, a modern building provides a 3D reconstruction of the amphitheater, helping visitors visualize how it looked in its prime.

For those interested in ancient history and Roman architecture, the Palais Gallien is a must-see. Open daily with free admission, it's a budget-friendly stop for any traveler. Guided tours are available, offering deeper insights into its historical significance. Don't miss the chance to explore this unique part of Bordeaux's rich heritage and imagine life in the city nearly 2,000 years ago.

Historical Walking Tours

Bordeaux offers some incredible historical walking tours in 2024 that will immerse you in the city's rich past. A popular option is the Bordeaux Old Town Walking Tour, which takes you through the heart of the city's historical sites, including the awe-inspiring Saint-André Cathedral, the medieval Porte Cailhau, and the stunning Place de la Bourse. This tour, led by expert local guides, typically lasts around two hours, allowing you to discover Bordeaux's history and architecture in a personal and engaging way.

Another fantastic option is the Bordeaux Highlights Walking Tour, which runs in the evenings. This allows you to experience the city under its magical night lights, making stops at key landmarks like the Grosse Cloche and the Grand Theatre. The guides bring history to life with captivating stories of Bordeaux's past, making this an enjoyable and informative way to explore.

For something different, consider the Mystery Walking Tour. Perfect for those who enjoy history with a twist, this tour explores myths, legends, and ghost stories of the medieval city, offering a thrilling and unusual perspective on Bordeaux's history.

CHAPTER 6: NEIGHBORHOODS TO EXPLORE

Saint-Pierre District: The Heart of Old Bordeaux

The Saint-Pierre District in Bordeaux is a must-visit neighborhood for anyone traveling to the city in 2024. This historic area is the heart of Old Bordeaux, where the city's medieval roots meet its modern charm. As you wander through the narrow, cobbled streets, you'll be walking in the footsteps of merchants and craftsmen who lived here centuries ago, giving you a true sense of the city's rich history.

One of the district's most iconic landmarks is the **Porte Cailhau**, a striking 15th-century gate that once served as the city's main entrance from the Garonne River. Today, it stands proudly at Place du Palais, a lively square perfect for grabbing a coffee or glass of wine while admiring the medieval architecture. For a local tip, try **Tutiac, Le Bistro Vignerons** near the gate it's a great spot to enjoy Bordeaux's famous wines.

The **Église Saint-Pierre**, located in the charming Place Saint-Pierre, is another must-see. This Gothic-style church dates back to the 12th century and is steeped in history. The surrounding square is quiet and picturesque, making it a great place to pause and soak in the atmosphere. For food lovers, the district is home to plenty of cozy restaurants and wine bars along **Rue des Faussets**. Whether you're craving traditional French cuisine or innovative modern dishes, there's something for every palate.

If you love shopping, Saint-Pierre has a mix of high-end boutiques and quirky antique shops, giving you plenty of options for finding unique souvenirs. Don't miss **Place du Parlement**, a beautiful square where you can relax and watch the world go by. The area truly comes alive in the evening, with lively bars and restaurants catering to both locals and tourists.

Touring the district is easy it's compact and walkable, with most attractions within a short stroll of each other. And if you're looking for the perfect spot to end your day, head to the **Miroir d'eau** at Place de la Bourse, just a stone's throw from Saint-Pierre. This giant water mirror reflects the elegant architecture of the city and is especially beautiful at sunset.

Whether you're a first-time visitor or a seasoned traveler, Saint-Pierre offers a captivating blend of history, culture, and modern French life.

Chartrons: The Wine Merchant District

Chartrons, Bordeaux's historic wine merchant district, offers visitors a perfect mix of heritage, culture, and local charm. Located just north of the city center, Chartrons was once the hub of Bordeaux's booming wine trade. Today, this neighborhood has transformed into a vibrant area with artisan boutiques, art galleries, and some of the best cafés in the city.

Start your visit to **Rue Notre Dame**, the heart of Chartrons. Here, you'll find an array of antique shops and trendy boutiques, blending Bordeaux's old-world charm with modern flair. It's an excellent place for both casual shopping and exploring local culture. Take your time browsing the street's independent stores, from vintage shops to fine jewelry and home décor.

One of the highlights of Chartrons is the **Bordeaux Wine and Trade Museum**. This museum offers a fascinating glimpse into the history of the area and Bordeaux's deep connection with the global wine industry. It's a must-visit for wine lovers who want to understand the roots of the region's wine-making traditions.

Make sure to stop by the **Place du Marché des Chartrons**, where every Sunday, a bustling open-air market springs to life. Here, you can mingle with locals, sample regional specialties like canelés and oysters, and enjoy fresh produce. It's also a great spot for a leisurely brunch or lunch with a view of the **Garonne River**.

For art lovers, Chartrons is home to several galleries, with the **CAPC Museum of Contemporary Art** being a highlight. The museum regularly hosts exhibitions featuring both local and international artists, making it a fantastic stop for those interested in Bordeaux's contemporary art scene.

Bastide: A Quieter Side of the City

Bastide, located on the right bank of the Garonne River, offers a serene escape from the bustling heart of Bordeaux. Once an industrial hub, the neighborhood has transformed into a charming and tranquil area perfect for those looking to experience Bordeaux at a slower pace.

The highlight of Bastide is its peaceful atmosphere, far removed from the busier parts of the city. Take a stroll through the **Jardin Botanique**, a beautiful botanical garden, ideal for picnics or quiet reflection. The garden showcases a variety of native plants and hosts seasonal exhibitions, making it a must-see for nature lovers.

Bastide is also home to the **Darwin Eco-District**, a fascinating blend of sustainability, creativity, and culture. This former military barracks has been repurposed into a dynamic space that features co-working areas, organic shops, and even a skatepark. You can grab a coffee at the eco-conscious café or explore the organic market, which highlights local, fresh produce. For those interested in sustainability, the Darwin district is a unique glimpse into Bordeaux's commitment to eco-friendly living.

While in Bastide, don't miss the chance to walk across the **Pont de Pierre**, the iconic bridge that connects this neighborhood to central Bordeaux. From the bridge, you'll have stunning views of the city's skyline. For a truly local experience, head to one of Bastide's hidden gems, **Le Siman**, a riverside restaurant where you can enjoy a meal with breathtaking views of the Garonne.

Bastide's mix of quiet charm, history, and modern innovation makes it a perfect spot for travelers looking to experience a different side of Bordeaux.

Saint-Michel: A Melting Pot of Cultures

Saint-Michel is one of Bordeaux's most lively and culturally diverse neighborhoods. Known locally as "Saint Mich," this area is a fusion of history and modern life. As you explore, you'll notice its Gothic roots anchored by the towering **Basilique Saint-Michel**, dating back to the 14th century, with its majestic spire offering stunning panoramic views of the city. Climbing its 228 steps is well worth the effort for sweeping views of Bordeaux from above.

But what truly sets Saint-Michel apart is its cultural mix. It's a neighborhood where North African, Middle Eastern, and European influences blend seamlessly, creating a unique atmosphere that feels both local and global. **Rue des Faures** is the heart of this melting pot, filled with small shops selling spices, tagine dishes, and Mediterranean treats. Don't miss **Bazar Istanbul**, a hidden gem where you can find everything from Persian spices to traditional teas.

The area comes alive at its various markets. Every Sunday, the **Brocante du Dimanche** brings over 80 vendors to the square, offering antiques, second-hand treasures, and collectibles. For food lovers, the **Marché des Capucins**, just a short walk away, is Bordeaux's largest daily market, where you can sample local dishes or enjoy international flavors like Moroccan tagines and Vietnamese pho.

If you're looking for a local food experience, head to **La Mère Michel**, a charming bistro that blends delicious crêpes with a vintage décor all for sale! For a more casual break, try **Café de la Fraternité** for a refreshing mint tea, a favorite drink among locals, reflecting the area's Maghreb influence.

Quinconces and its Monument

Quinconces, home to the famous Monument aux Girondins, is one of Bordeaux's most iconic landmarks. It is the heart of the city, featuring the largest square in France and one of the largest in Europe. If you're exploring Bordeaux in 2024 or beyond, this historic space is a must-see, combining rich history with a lively cultural scene.

The monument itself was erected to honor the Girondists, political figures during the French Revolution, and its detailed sculptures are truly impressive. The fountain's bronze horses and the towering spire topped with the statue of Liberty symbolize freedom and victory, making it a striking focal point. Walking through Quinconces is like stepping into a grand chapter of French history.

Aside from its historical significance, Quinconces is an active hub for cultural events. In 2024, it continues to host everything from antique fairs to open-air concerts, so there's always something happening. Twice a year, the square transforms into a bustling funfair, drawing both locals and tourists alike. If you're here in spring or autumn, don't miss the chance to experience this festive event.

For travelers seeking a more leisurely visit, the square is perfect for strolling under the shady trees planted in a quincunx formation—giving the area its name. There are also nearby cafés where you can relax and soak in the atmosphere. Try the nearby "Bar à Vin," a local favorite for sampling Bordeaux wines, or *"Nulle Part Ailleurs"* for a cozy, laid-back meal.

Getting to Quinconces is simple, thanks to its location on Bordeaux's efficient tram network (lines B and C stop here). From here, you can easily explore the riverfront or the neighboring Jardin Public, making Quinconces an ideal starting point for your Bordeaux escapade.

CHAPTER 7: LOCAL FOOD AND DRINK

Essential Bordeaux Dishes to Try (Canelé, Entrecôte à la Bordelaise)

Bordeaux is a city known not only for its world-class wines but also for its rich culinary heritage. When visiting this beautiful city, trying the local food is a must. Here's a guide to the essential dishes you should savor during your stay in Bordeaux:

1. Entrecôte à la Bordelaise

This iconic dish is a must-try for meat lovers. Entrecôte à la Bordelaise is a ribeye steak served with a rich Bordelaise sauce made from Bordeaux red wine, bone marrow, shallots, and herbs. The sauce enhances the succulent flavors of the beef, creating a perfect balance between the meaty texture and the deep, wine-infused richness. Locals often enjoy this dish with crispy French fries or sautéed potatoes on the side.

To truly experience Bordeaux like a local, pair this dish with a bold red wine from the region, such as a Médoc or Saint-Émilion. You'll find excellent versions of Entrecôte à la Bordelaise in many traditional brasseries across the city, including **Le Chapon Fin** and **Le Bouchon Bordelais**, where they master the art of this classic dish.

2. Canelé

For those with a sweet tooth, the Canelé is an absolute delight. This small pastry, crispy on the outside and soft on the inside, is made from a rich, custard-like batter flavored with vanilla and rum. Originating from Bordeaux in the 18th century, it's traditionally baked in copper molds to achieve its perfect caramelized crust. While Canelés can be found all over France, tasting them in their birthplace is a special experience. Locals often enjoy them with a glass of sweet Bordeaux wine like Sauternes. You can find the best Canelés at **La Toque Cuivrée** and **Baillardran**, two shops renowned for their authentic, irresistible versions of this treat.

3. Lamproie à la Bordelaise

A more adventurous dish, Lamproie à la Bordelaise, is a stew made from lamprey, a type of jawless fish, slow-cooked in red wine with leeks, garlic, and bacon. This dish dates back centuries and is considered a delicacy in the Bordeaux region. It's often served with crusty bread or potatoes to soak up the rich, flavorful sauce. For a truly local experience, try this dish in traditional restaurants such as **La Tupina**, where regional dishes are crafted with care and respect for tradition.

4. Oysters from Arcachon Bay

Bordeaux's proximity to the Atlantic coast means that seafood is a key part of the local cuisine. The oysters from Arcachon Bay are among the finest in France, renowned for their fresh, briny flavor. Served raw on the half-shell with a splash of lemon or mignonette sauce, these oysters are a favorite at seafood markets and restaurants alike. For an authentic experience, head to the **Marché des Capucins**, Bordeaux's vibrant market, where you can enjoy freshly shucked oysters alongside a glass of crisp white wine, like a Graves or Entre-Deux-Mers.

5. Cèpes de Bordeaux

Bordeaux is also known for its seasonal produce, particularly **cèpes** (porcini mushrooms). These meaty, flavorful mushrooms are usually pan-fried with garlic, parsley, and butter, offering a delicious, earthy taste. Cèpes are typically served as a side dish or even the main attraction for vegetarians. They pair beautifully with a Merlot-dominated red wine. You can find them in season at many local restaurants and markets during the late summer and fall.

By sampling these iconic dishes, you'll get a true taste of Bordeaux's culinary heritage. Each dish tells a story of the region's deep connection to its land, traditions, and, of course, its famous wine. To explore more and make the most of your culinary journey in Bordeaux.

Best Cafés and Bakeries in Bordeaux

1. L'Alchimiste Café Boutique

Located at 12 Rue Vieille Tour, this café is a must for any coffee enthusiast. Known for its artisanal coffee roasts, L'Alchimiste offers a minimalist yet cozy setting where the focus is entirely on the coffee experience. The café also hosts workshops, perfect for those who want to dive deeper into the art of coffee making. While you won't find food here, the rich aromas and expertly crafted brews more than makeup for it.

2. La Pelle Café

At 29 Rue Notre-Dame, La Pelle offers a unique experience combining international flavors with Bordeaux's rich café culture. The owner's background in both Brazilian and Italian coffee traditions gives the café a multicultural twist. You can enjoy a delicious brunch or snack while sipping on freshly roasted coffee. This spot is loved for its casual vibe and diverse menu.

3. Café Piha

For a more laid-back atmosphere, head to Café Piha at 69 Rue des Ayres. This café is known for its specialty roasts and comfortable seating, encouraging you to linger. The café also hosts workshops where you can learn about coffee roasting and brewing techniques. Their baked goods are a treat, pairing perfectly with their house-blend coffee.

4. Maison Perrin

Maison Perrin is a family-run bakery with locations across Bordeaux, but its original shop is a must-visit. The combination of expertly baked breads, pastries, chocolates, and even ice cream makes this bakery a favorite. Their selection of sandwiches and quiches is perfect for a quick bite before diving into their dessert offerings.

5. Au Pétrin Moissagais

One of Bordeaux's oldest bakeries, Au Pétrin Moissagais, located at 72 Cours de la Martinique, has been in operation since the 1760s. The bakery is famed for its traditional Gascogne-style bread, baked in a wood-fired oven that dates back centuries. It's a slice of history with every bite.

6. La Diplomate

This charming tea house at 32 Rue Parlement Saint-Pierre offers a cozy retreat in the heart of Bordeaux. La Diplomate is adored for its wide selection of teas, homemade pastries, and delightful atmosphere. It's the perfect spot to relax on a rainy day while indulging in scones or their signature tea blends

7. Pâtisserie du Cours

Located in the heart of Bordeaux, Pâtisserie du Cours specializes in traditional French desserts, including éclairs, tartes tatins, and macarons. Their chocolate mousse cake, topped with fresh berries, is a standout. It's a great place to stop after exploring the city, offering a sweet treat that perfectly complements a day of sightseeing.

These cafés and bakeries provide an authentic taste of Bordeaux. Whether you're looking for a quick snack, a leisurely brunch, or a place to unwind with a coffee, each spot offers a distinct experience that captures the city's charm. If you're planning to visit Bordeaux in 2025, make sure to stop by these places for a memorable culinary journey.

Top Restaurants for Fine Dining

When visiting Bordeaux, a must-do for food lovers is experiencing its top restaurants known for fine dining. As of 2024, the city boasts several Michelin-starred establishments, where dining is not just about food, but an art form. Here's a curated list of some of the finest dining experiences that you should consider for your trip in 2025.

1. Le Gabriel

Located in the heart of Place de la Bourse, Le Gabriel is a two-in-one venue with both a casual dining space and its fine dining gem, L'Observatoire. It is renowned for its exquisite seafood dishes and breathtaking views of the Garonne River. Chef Alexandre Baumard, who has won numerous accolades, crafts elegant dishes using the freshest ingredients from the region. The restaurant offers an exceptional seasonal menu where you can savor innovative twists on classic French cuisine. For a truly memorable evening, try their tasting menu paired with some of the best Bordeaux wines.

2. Le Pressoir d'Argent – Gordon Ramsay

This two-Michelin-starred restaurant, located in the iconic InterContinental Bordeaux, offers a luxurious and refined dining experience. Helmed by Gordon Ramsay, the restaurant specializes in seafood, with its signature dish being the Brittany lobster pressed using a silver lobster press, one of the few in the world. Ramsay's team brings British flair to French fine dining, creating a blend of bold flavors and delicate textures. Reservations are highly recommended due to the high demand, especially for their multi-course tasting menus.

3. La Grande Maison de Bernard Magrez

This restaurant offers an experience that fuses gastronomy with art. The elegant setting of this restaurant is complemented by the genius of Chef Pierre Gagnaire, known for his daring and artistic culinary creations. Expect a symphony of flavors, with dishes that highlight regional products, such as foie gras and prime cuts of beef. This Michelin-starred gem is ideal for those looking to experience the pinnacle of Bordeaux's culinary scene.

4. Le Pavillon des Boulevards

Located a bit outside the city center, this restaurant is the perfect blend of tradition and modernity. Chef Thomas Morel, an alumnus of renowned French kitchens, creates a seasonal menu inspired by local produce. The dishes are as visually stunning as they are flavorful, and the peaceful garden terrace offers a relaxing atmosphere. A meal here is not just food but a sensory experience, especially in the warmer months when you can dine al fresco.

5. Influences

For something a bit different, check out Influences, a unique blend of French and Californian cuisine run by an American-French duo. The menu here is always a

surprise, offering guests an adventurous dining experience. Opt for the five-course tasting menu with wine pairings for a full immersion into the innovative fusion of flavors. Be sure to book ahead, as this spot fills up fast.

Insider Tips

To make the most of your fine dining experiences in Bordeaux, booking in advance is key, especially for Michelin-starred restaurants, as tables fill up quickly, particularly on weekends. If you're visiting during the summer, inquire about special seasonal menus or wine-pairing events that many of these restaurants offer. For wine lovers, combining a meal with a wine-tasting tour in the nearby vineyards adds another layer to the experience.

Dining in Bordeaux is not just about eating, it's about indulging in the city's rich culture and history through food.

Markets to Visit (Marché des Capucins, Marché des Grands Hommes)

If you're looking to experience Bordeaux's vibrant food scene, two markets stand out for their variety, charm, and reflection of the city's rich culinary heritage: **Marché des Capucins** and **Marché des Grands Hommes**. Visiting these markets offers a chance to taste local flavors and mingle with locals, and they are must-sees on any food lover's itinerary for 2025.

Marché des Capucins is often referred to as the "stomach of Bordeaux," and for good reason. Located in the Saint-Michel district, this bustling market has been serving residents since the 18th century. Open six days a week, from Tuesday to Sunday, it's a sensory experience you won't forget. As you walk through the market, the colors and aromas of fresh produce, cheeses, and meats greet you, while vendors eagerly share their specialties. Be sure to sample the **canelés**, the caramelized pastries Bordeaux is famous for, or sit down with a plate of **fresh oysters** and a glass of white wine an iconic local pairing.

One of the things that makes Marché des Capucins special is its multicultural flair. You'll find stalls offering everything from traditional French charcuterie to Moroccan tagines and Spanish tapas. The atmosphere is lively, and locals love to grab breakfast or brunch at one of the market's many eateries. If you visit on a weekend, expect a vibrant scene, with tourists and locals alike enjoying a glass of wine at **Le Bistro Poulette** or savoring mussels at **Le Guet À Pan**. Plan your visit early in the morning to get the best produce and avoid the crowds. This market is open from 5:30 AM on weekends, making it a perfect stop for a morning adventure.

For a more upscale and refined market experience, head over to **Marché des Grands Hommes**, located in the heart of the city's Golden Triangle. Housed in a neoclassical rotunda, this market blends history with modern elegance. Though smaller and more polished than Capucins, Grands Hommes offers high-quality, fresh produce and artisanal goods.

You can find gourmet cheeses, meats, and delicacies from around the region, perfect for crafting a luxurious picnic or bringing home unique souvenirs.

Marché des Grands Hommes is also known for its chic ambiance, attracting both locals and tourists who are seeking top-tier produce and a less hectic shopping experience. If you're interested in Bordeaux's renowned wines, there are vendors here who specialize in bottles from the nearby vineyards. The market is open daily, including Sundays, though it's best to visit in the late morning or early afternoon to avoid the quieter hours when vendors are just setting up.

No matter which market you choose, you'll walk away with a deeper appreciation for Bordeaux's rich culinary culture. From the hustle of Capucins to the refinement of Grands Hommes, each market has its unique flavor and charm. If you're planning your visit to Bordeaux, these markets are not to be missed. They capture the spirit of the city and provide you with an unforgettable taste of the local life.

Local Spirits and Beverages Beyond Wine

When you think of Bordeaux, wine undoubtedly comes to mind, but this beautiful region offers much more for those who want to explore beyond its famous vineyards. Bordeaux is experiencing a surge in craft spirits, local beers, and non-alcoholic beverages, making it a vibrant destination for anyone curious about its lesser-known drinks. Whether you're a fan of spirits or looking for unique, non-alcoholic options, there's something for everyone to enjoy.

Craft Spirits

Bordeaux is home to a growing craft spirits scene that reflects the region's rich heritage and commitment to quality. While Cognac and Armagnac remain classic favorites, newer distilleries are producing exceptional craft gins and whiskeys. One standout is Moon Harbour Distillery, located right in the heart of Bordeaux. Moon Harbour specializes in whiskey that captures the essence of the region, incorporating local ingredients and aging processes that give it a distinct flavor. Visitors can tour the distillery and learn about the production process while sampling some of their unique whiskies.

Another rising star is Bordeaux Distilling Company, which focuses on craft gin, rum, and even vodka. Their small-batch gin is infused with botanicals that reflect the flavors of Bordeaux. You can sample these spirits at local bars or distilleries, where the emphasis is always on craftsmanship and creativity.

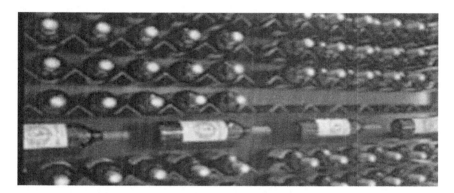

Local Beers

Bordeaux's beer scene has grown considerably in recent years, offering an excellent alternative for those looking to taste something beyond wine. Craft breweries such as Azimut Brasserie and Brasserie du Mascaret are at the forefront of this movement. Azimut Brasserie, known for its experimental approach, offers a range of beers that use locally sourced ingredients, creating brews that are a true reflection of Bordeaux's terroir. From IPAs to pale ales, you'll find a wide variety of styles to choose from. Brasserie du Mascaret, located near the Garonne River, focuses on traditional brewing methods while still keeping things fresh and innovative.

For beer lovers, Bordeaux's burgeoning craft beer festivals and taprooms provide the perfect opportunity to explore. Many bars and pubs in the city now have rotating taps that feature local and regional beers, making it easy to dive into Bordeaux's beer culture.

Non-Alcoholic Beverages

The non-alcoholic beverage scene in Bordeaux is also thriving, especially with the global rise in mindful drinking. Trendy non-alcoholic spirits and mocktails are now a common offering in many Bordeaux bars and restaurants. Brands like *Les Bienheureux* offer alcohol-free spirits that mimic the complexity of traditional beverages, allowing non-drinkers to enjoy a crafted drink experience. Look out for creative non-alcoholic cocktails that use ingredients like herbs, local fruits, and spices, providing a refreshing alternative that still feels indulgent.

Many cafés also serve regional specialties like locally brewed kombucha or herbal teas that highlight the unique flavors of southwestern France. These are perfect options for those who prefer a sober experience but still want to enjoy the local culture.

Pairing Drinks with Local Cuisine

To truly experience Bordeaux's food and drink culture, pair these craft beverages with local dishes. Try a gin and tonic from Bordeaux Distilling Company alongside fresh oysters, or enjoy a craft beer with a plate of local charcuterie. For non-alcoholic options, herbal teas or alcohol-free spirits pair beautifully with lighter fare such as goat cheese salad or seafood.

Exploring Bordeaux's local spirits, beers, and non-alcoholic drinks will add an exciting dimension to your trip.

CHAPTER 8: DAY TRIPS FROM BORDEAUX

Saint-Emilion: Medieval Village and Vineyards

If you're staying in Bordeaux, a day trip to Saint-Émilion is an absolute must. This medieval village, just 35 minutes by train from Bordeaux, offers a rich blend of history, breathtaking architecture, and world-renowned vineyards. Listed as a UNESCO World Heritage site since 1999, Saint-Émilion feels like stepping back in time, with cobblestone streets, ancient churches, and rows of lush vineyards rolling out across the horizon.

What to See in Saint-Émilion

Start your day with a visit to the iconic **Monolithic Church**. This incredible underground church, carved out of limestone in the 12th century, is the largest of its kind in Europe. Its towering bell tower rises 68 meters above the village and offers a panoramic view of the vineyards and rooftops. Be sure to book a guided tour in advance, as access to the underground portions is restricted to tours only, and these can fill up fast, especially in the high season

After exploring the church, take a walk to the **King's Tower**. Climbing its 196 steps may be a challenge, but the view from the top is unbeatable, offering sweeping vistas of Saint-Émilion's vineyards. Another notable site is the **Cloister of the Cordeliers**, where you can enjoy a glass of Crémant, a sparkling wine produced in the region while strolling through the beautiful gardens.

Wine Tasting and Vineyards

Saint-Émilion is famous for its wine, particularly **Premier Grand Cru Classé** wines. You'll find estates like **Château Ausone** and **Château Cheval Blanc**, which are world-renowned for their Merlot and Cabernet Franc blends. Many of these châteaux offer guided tours of their vineyards and cellars, followed by tastings of their exquisite wines

If you're more adventurous, consider renting an **e-bike** and cycling through the vineyards. This allows you to cover more ground while enjoying the fresh air and scenic countryside. Many e-bike tours also include stops at several wineries, giving you the chance to sample wines and learn about the region's winemaking process

For those who prefer a more leisurely experience, picnic options are available at some wineries, where you can enjoy local fare paired with a glass of wine amidst the vines. Booking a picnic at estates like **Clos des Abbesses** will give you a memorable, intimate experience.

Tips for a Smooth Visit

If you're planning a summer visit, remember to make restaurant and tour reservations well in advance, as Saint-Émilion can be quite popular during peak travel months. For food, **Logis de la Cadene**, a Michelin-starred restaurant, offers a gourmet experience, while **L'Envers du Décor** provides a laid-back atmosphere with exceptional food and wine.

As your day draws to a close, take a moment to relax by the vineyards or enjoy a final glass of wine in one of the village's charming squares. The beauty of Saint-Émilion is that it offers both relaxation and adventure, making it the perfect day trip for anyone visiting Bordeaux.

Arcachon Bay: Dune du Pilat and Oyster Farms

A day trip to Arcachon Bay from Bordeaux is an experience you won't want to miss. Just an hour's drive or train ride from the city, Arcachon Bay offers an escape into nature's beauty, with the stunning Dune du Pilat and the region's famous oyster farms providing an unforgettable day out.

Dune du Pilat

Your first stop in Arcachon Bay should be the Dune du Pilat, Europe's tallest dune. Standing at 102 meters (and constantly shifting due to the wind), it's a breathtaking natural wonder. Climbing to the top is an adventure in itself. During the high season (late May to early November), wooden stairs are set up to make the climb easier. If you visit in the off-season or want a more physical challenge, you can hike directly up the sand. Once you reach the summit, you're rewarded with a panoramic view that's nothing short of spectacular. To one side, you'll see the Atlantic Ocean stretching endlessly toward the horizon. On the other, the lush Landes Forest extends for miles. It's the perfect place to take in the beauty of nature, and many visitors spend hours exploring the dune and its surrounding areas.

For those feeling adventurous, sliding down the sandy slopes or enjoying a picnic with a view is a must.

Oyster Farms in Gujan-Mestras

After a morning at the Dune du Pilat, head to Gujan-Mestras, the oyster capital of Arcachon Bay. This small town is renowned for its oyster farms, which have been a staple of the region for centuries. Here, you can take a tour of the oyster farms, learning about the delicate art of oyster farming directly from the locals. Many farms offer guided tours where you can see the process firsthand from oyster beds to shucking and finish with a tasting of the freshest oysters you'll ever have. It's a great opportunity to immerse yourself in local traditions and experience the pride that the oyster farmers have for their craft.

Don't leave without enjoying a seafood lunch at one of the charming waterside restaurants. Many spots, like those in the picturesque village of L'Herbe on Cap Ferret, offer freshly harvested oysters paired with a glass of crisp white wine. If you're not a fan of oysters, the restaurants also serve a variety of other seafood dishes like mussels, shrimp, and fish, ensuring that everyone can find something to enjoy.

Boat Tours and Nature Reserves

For an even deeper experience of Arcachon Bay, consider taking a boat tour. Many operators offer short boat trips that take you around the bay, including visits to the **Banc d'Arguin**, a nature reserve that lies just off the coast. This island of sandbanks is a haven for birds, making it an ideal stop for nature lovers. You'll also have the opportunity to spot traditional oyster boats at work, a sight that ties the region's beauty to its longstanding traditions.

For an authentic taste of the region, be sure to include this trip in your itinerary.

Médoc Wine Route

If you're staying in Bordeaux and want to immerse yourself in the heart of one of the world's most famous wine regions, a day trip along the Médoc Wine Route is a must. Stretching between the Gironde estuary and the Atlantic coast, the Médoc region is renowned for its prestigious vineyards, breathtaking scenery, and châteaux that produce some of the finest wines in the world. In 2024, this route remains a timeless journey, offering visitors an authentic and unforgettable experience.

The Journey

Starting from Bordeaux, the Médoc Wine Route is best explored by car or bike. The D2 road, also known as the "Route des Châteaux," takes you through 131 kilometers of vineyards and picturesque villages. Whether you choose to drive or cycle, the path is marked, making it easy to navigate. If you prefer a more leisurely approach, several tour operators offer guided trips, some even picking you up directly from your hotel in Bordeaux.

Must-Visit Châteaux

The Médoc is home to some of the world's most famous wine estates, known for their impressive architecture and rich history.

Key stops include:

- **Château Margaux**: Often called the "Versailles of the Médoc," this château is not only architecturally stunning but also produces one of the region's premier Grand Cru wines. Tours are by appointment only, and while tastings are limited to professionals, the experience of visiting this legendary estate is unforgettable.

- **Château d'Agassac**: Located just 20 kilometers from Bordeaux, this charming château is a great place to start your Médoc tour. It offers an in-depth look at wine production and its beautiful setting makes for the perfect introduction to the region

- **Château Pichon Baron**: This stunning estate stands out for its unique design and world-class wines. Here, you can take guided tours that include a visit to the cellars, the vineyards, and of course, wine tastings.

Wine-Tasting Experiences

A visit to the Médoc wouldn't be complete without indulging in wine tastings. Most châteaux offer guided tours that walk you through the vineyards, cellars, and production processes, followed by tastings of their finest wines. Be sure to try the region's famous Cabernet Sauvignon and Merlot blends, which have earned Médoc its legendary reputation. Several estates also offer food pairings, enhancing the tasting experience.

Exploring by Bike

For the more adventurous, cycling through the Médoc is a popular option. The **Vélodyssée cycle path** stretches across the vineyards, offering a scenic way to explore the region at your own pace. With more than 120 kilometers of bike paths, you can stop at various châteaux for tastings, picnic by the Gironde estuary, and enjoy the peaceful countryside.

Tips for Visiting

- **Best Time to Visit**: While you can visit the Médoc year-round, spring and autumn are ideal times. Spring offers milder weather and fewer crowds, while autumn gives you a chance to witness the harvest and experience the vineyards at their busiest.

- **Make Appointments**: Many of the more prestigious châteaux require bookings for tours and tastings, so plan your visits.

- **What to Bring**: If you're cycling, bring a hat, sunscreen, and plenty of water, especially during the warmer months. If you're visiting by car, don't forget a jacket, as cellar tours can be cool.

Cognac: The World of Brandy

If you're planning a trip to Bordeaux, a visit to Cognac should be at the top of your list. Just 75 miles (about 1.5 hours by train or car) north of Bordeaux, Cognac is known worldwide for its iconic brandy. This picturesque town is the birthplace of Cognac brandy, and it offers much more than just tastings it's deep into centuries-old traditions, craftsmanship, and history that make this day trip unforgettable.

Your adventure begins in the heart of Cognac's old town. With its cobbled streets, half-timbered houses, and riverside walks along the Charente, this charming town will captivate you from the moment you arrive. The Château Royal de Cognac, a grand fortress that dates back to the 10th century, is a must-visit. Not only was it the birthplace of King François I, but today it is home to the Cognac brand Baron Otard. During a guided tour, you'll discover the castle's rich history and enjoy tastings of premium Cognac like XO Gold or Extra 1795, right from the cellars of the château.

But no visit to Cognac would be complete without learning about the intricate process behind this famed spirit. The town boasts some of the world's most prestigious Cognac houses Rémy Martin, Hennessy, Martell, and Camus all of which offer guided tours in English. Each tour will walk you through the full distillation process, from grape to glass, giving you insight into what makes each house unique. At Rémy Martin, for example, you can explore their historic cellars and even enjoy gourmet pairings with local cuisine. Camus, another standout, uses a special distillation process that heightens the fruity aromas of their Cognac, creating a richer tasting experience.

One of the highlights of a Cognac Day trip is, of course, the tastings. Whether you're sampling at Hennessy's riverside cellars or creating your blend at Camus during a masterclass, the experience is unparalleled. Each house offers tastings of their best creations, with options ranging from VS (Very Special) Cognac to XO (Extra Old), depending on the tour you choose.

For a more intimate experience, consider visiting smaller family-owned producers like Domaine Pasquet, known for their organic Cognac and welcoming atmosphere. Here, you'll not only learn about small-batch production but also taste truly handcrafted Cognac, offering a more personal touch compared to the larger houses.

Beyond the spirit, Cognac's rich history and tranquil landscapes make it a perfect destination. Take a stroll through its vineyards or visit the Musée des Arts du Cognac to dive deeper into the region's brandy-making heritage.

A day trip to Cognac isn't just about the brandy it's a cultural journey that blends history, craftsmanship, and the beauty of French heritage. For any visitor to Bordeaux, this is an essential experience that will leave you with lasting memories and a newfound appreciation for one of the world's finest spirits.

Dordogne Valley: Castles and Caves

If you're planning a day trip from Bordeaux in 2024, the Dordogne Valley should be at the top of your list. This region is a treasure trove of stunning landscapes, medieval castles, and ancient caves, making it the perfect escape into history and natural beauty. Whether you're a lover of architecture, adventure, or prehistoric art, the Dordogne has something magical to offer.

Castles of the Dordogne

Your first stop should be the Château de Beynac, a fortress perched high above the Dordogne River. As you approach the castle, you'll be amazed by its commanding view over the valley, where you can almost feel the weight of history. Dating back to the 12th century, this castle was once home to Richard the Lionheart and is known for its imposing towers and ramparts. You can explore its medieval chambers, the guardroom, and even the kitchen with its impressive fireplace. The château is open year-round, and it's easy to reach from nearby Sarlat. Be sure to take in the panoramic view from the terrace it's breathtaking.

Another must-see is Château de Castelnaud, just a short drive away. This castle, now a museum of medieval warfare, is home to an impressive collection of armor and weaponry. It's an educational experience for both adults and kids, with displays that bring the region's tumultuous history to life. The nearby Château des Milandes is also worth visiting, especially if you're interested in learning about the life of Josephine Baker, the famous American-born entertainer who made it her home.

Exploring the Caves

The Dordogne Valley is just as famous for its underground treasures. The Lascaux Cave, located in Montignac, is one of the most well-known prehistoric sites in the world. Although the original cave is closed to preserve its ancient paintings, you can visit Lascaux IV, a painstakingly created replica. This state-of-the-art museum allows you to experience the 20,000-year-old cave art up close and learn about the lives of the people who created it. For a deeper prehistory, consider visiting the Font-de-Gaume Cave, one of the last caves in France still open to the public that features original polychrome paintings.

Outdoor Activities

A day trip to the Dordogne isn't complete without some outdoor adventure. The Dordogne River is ideal for canoeing, offering a peaceful way to take in the valley's scenic beauty. As you paddle down the river, you'll glide past towering cliffs and villages that seem frozen in time, like the medieval Domme, which sits perched on a hill offering stunning views. Several local operators offer canoe rentals, and you can enjoy a leisurely afternoon soaking in the natural surroundings.

Tasting the Dordogne

While in the Dordogne, you must sample the region's renowned cuisine. Stop at a local market in Sarlat-la-Canéda for specialties like foie gras, truffles, and walnut delicacies. Enjoy a meal at a farm inn (ferme auberge), where you'll savor traditional Périgord dishes prepared with locally sourced ingredients. The food here truly reflects the region's rich culinary heritage.

A day trip to the Dordogne from Bordeaux will leave you with unforgettable memories of castles, caves, and culinary delights. It's an experience that seamlessly blends history, adventure, and relaxation perfect for any traveler seeking a glimpse of the true beauty of France.

CHAPTER 9: ACCOMMODATION OPTIONS

Luxury Hotels in Bordeaux

InterContinental Bordeaux - Le Grand Hotel

Location: 2-5 Place de la Comédie, 33000 Bordeaux, France

Phone: +33 5 57 30 43 04

Website: bordeaux.intercontinental.com

Price Range: From €450 per night

The InterContinental Bordeaux - Le Grand Hotel is the perfect embodiment of French luxury and elegance. Situated in the heart of Bordeaux, this 5-star hotel offers more than just a stay; it provides an exceptional experience of opulence.

The hotel is renowned for its **rooftop spa**, featuring a heated pool, a sauna, and panoramic views of Bordeaux's skyline, including the iconic Grand Théâtre. The hotel also houses the **Guerlain Spa**, where you can indulge in premium treatments, including massages and rejuvenating therapies.

Le Pressoir d'Argent Gordon Ramsay, a two-star Michelin restaurant within the hotel, serves exquisite French dishes that reflect local produce. Guests can enjoy seafood specialties like Breton lobster and fine desserts prepared by top chefs. For a more casual dining experience, **Le Bordeaux restaurant** offers a taste of southwestern French cuisine with contemporary twists on traditional recipes.

Other amenities include:

- 130 elegant rooms and suites, each featuring classic French decor with modern touches

- **Fitness center** with state-of-the-art equipment

- **Valet parking** (€45/day)

- **Pet-friendly services**

- Multiple event and conference rooms for business meetings or special occasions

This hotel is ideal for luxury travelers looking for a high-end experience in the heart of Bordeaux, with world-class dining and wellness services

Mondrian Bordeaux Les Carmes

Location: 5 Rue de la Faïencerie, 33300 Bordeaux, France

Phone: +33 5 56 00 00 00

Website: anrdoezrs.net

Price Range: From €400 per night

Located in the trendy Chartrons district, the **Mondrian Bordeaux Les Carmes** is a luxurious 5-star hotel, offering a contemporary and artistic vibe. The hotel is housed in a former wine cellar, blending history with modern luxury. Its 97 rooms and suites are designed with stylish, modern interiors that provide both comfort and sophistication, many of them offering **terraces with city views**.

One of the hotel's standout features is its **Japanese restaurant**, where you can enjoy innovative Japanese cuisine in a chic, alfresco setting. The hotel also has a **terrace bar** that serves craft cocktails and Japanese sake, ideal for relaxing after a day of exploring the city.

Amenities include:

- **Indoor heated pool** with a sauna and Hammam

- **Spa and wellness center** offering personalized treatments

- **Fitness center**

- Meeting and event spaces for corporate gatherings

This hotel is perfect for travelers who want a balance of luxury and modernity, with easy access to Bordeaux's cultural spots

Les Sources De Caudalie

Location: Chemin de Smith Haut Lafitte, 33650 Martillac, France

Phone: +33 5 57 83 83 83

Website: sources-caudalie.com

Price Range: From €500 per night

Nestled in the vineyards of Martillac, **Les Sources De Caudalie** is a luxury countryside retreat just a short 20-minute drive from Bordeaux city center. This 5-star hotel specializes in **vinotherapy**, offering spa treatments that use grape and vine extracts. The hotel is surrounded by the Château Smith Haut Lafitte vineyards, making it an ideal spot for wine lovers.

The hotel offers **two gourmet restaurants**, including **La Grand'Vigne**, a Michelin-starred venue where guests can enjoy gourmet dishes inspired by the local terroir. For a more relaxed atmosphere, **La Table du Lavoir** offers traditional French dishes in a cozy setting.

Amenities include:

- **Indoor and outdoor pools**

- **Tennis court** and **pitch & putt golf course**

- **Free bike rentals** to explore the surrounding vineyards

- Extensive wine-tasting sessions

- **Cooking classes** and vineyard tours

This hotel is perfect for luxury travelers seeking relaxation in a scenic, wine-filled setting.

Yndo Hotel

Location: 108 Rue Abbé de l'Épée, 33000 Bordeaux, France

Phone: +33 5 56 23 88 88

Website: yndohotelbordeaux.com

Price Range: From €350 per night

Yndo Hotel is a boutique 5-star hotel set in a 19th-century

mansion located in the heart of Bordeaux. This charming hotel offers just 12 uniquely designed rooms and suites, each decorated with a blend of contemporary art and classic elegance. The hotel prides itself on offering personalized service, making every stay unique and tailored to each guest's needs.

Guests can dine at the **hotel's exclusive restaurant**, which offers seasonal dishes made from local ingredients. The tranquil **garden and terrace** are perfect for enjoyin g a morning coffee or an evening cocktail.

Amenities include:

- **Designer rooms** with custom decor and high-end furniture

- **In-room dining service**

- **Exclusive garden area**

- **Private parking**

Yndo Hotel is ideal for travelers looking for an intimate, personalized experience in the center of Bordeaux.

Villas Foch

Location: 25 Cours du Maréchal Foch, 33000 Bordeaux, France

Phone: +33 5 57 35 66 00

Website: villasfoch.com

Price Range: From €400 per night

Villas Foch is a recent addition to Bordeaux's luxury scene, housed in two meticulously restored 17th and 18th-century mansions. This 5-star boutique hotel offers 20 rooms, providing an exclusive and private experience. The hotel blends historical architecture with modern luxury, creating a serene environment in the heart of Bordeaux.

Amenities include:

- **Spa with an indoor pool**

- **Fitness center**

- **Bar and lounge**

- **Private garden**

- Personalized concierge services for dining and tour recommendations

This hotel is ideal for luxury travelers who prefer a quiet, intimate stay with access to modern amenities.

Mid-Range Hotels:

Renaissance Bordeaux Hotel

Location: 16 Rue de Gironde, 33000 Bordeaux, France

Phone: +33 5 35 31 40 40

Website: renaissance-hotels.marriott.com

Price Range: From €180 per night

The **Renaissance Bordeaux Hotel** is located in the trendy Old Docks area, offering a modern and stylish stay. This 4-star hotel is known for its **rooftop pool**, which provides stunning views of the Garonne River and the Bordeaux skyline. With 149 well-appointed rooms featuring floor-to-ceiling windows, guests can enjoy luxurious touches with a modern twist. The **Gina Restaurant & Bar** serves Italian-inspired cuisine throughout the day, making it an excellent option for dining after exploring the city.

Amenities include:

- **Rooftop pool** with panoramic city views

- **Fitness center**

- **Business center** for travelers working on the go

- **Conference rooms** for events and meetings

This hotel is a great choice for both leisure and business travelers, offering comfort, modern amenities, and proximity to the Bassins à Flot and other nearby attractions.

Marty Hotel Bordeaux, Tapestry Collection by Hilton

Location: 153 Rue Georges Bonnac, 33000 Bordeaux, France

Phone: +33 5 57 87 70 70

Website: hilton.com

Price Range: From €160 per night

Located in Bordeaux's revitalized **Mériadeck district**, the Marty Hotel offers a boutique experience with a mid-century modern design. The interiors are vibrant, featuring art installations curated by local artists. With 61 rooms, guests can expect cozy, stylish spaces with contemporary touches. The hotel's **cocktail bar** is a hotspot for both visitors and locals, offering a wide selection of regional wines and craft cocktails.

Amenities include:

- **Art gallery-inspired interiors**

- **Cocktail bar** with a focus on regional wines

- **Pet-friendly accommodations**

- **proximity to tram lines** for easy city access

Marty Hotel is an excellent mid-range choice for travelers looking for modern comforts and a touch of art and culture.

Hôtel de Sèze

Location: 23 Allées de Tourny, 33000 Bordeaux, France

Phone: +33 5 56 14 16 16

Website: hotel-de-seze.com

Price Range: From €200 per night

This charming 4-star hotel boasts a central location, just a stone's throw from the **Esplanade des Quinconces** and the historic heart of Bordeaux. **Hôtel de Sèze** offers 55 rooms, each with a classic French decor that exudes elegance and warmth. The hotel's **spa facilities** include a hammam and jacuzzi, offering a relaxing retreat after a day of sightseeing. Guests can also enjoy dining at the hotel's **Le Comptoir de Sèze**, which serves traditional French cuisine.

Amenities include:

- **Spa and wellness center** with hammam and jacuzzi

- **In-house restaurant**

- **Private parking**

- **Golf simulator** for sports enthusiasts

This hotel is perfect for travelers who appreciate classic French decor and a serene, centrally located retreat

Hotel Indigo Bordeaux Centre Chartrons

Location: 18 Parvis des Chartrons, 33000 Bordeaux, France

Phone: +33 5 56 01 01 01

Website: ihg.com

Price Range: From €170 per night

Hotel Indigo Bordeaux is situated in the bohemian **Chartrons district**, known for its galleries and antique shops. This 4-star hotel offers a chic, modern stay with stunning views of the Garonne River from its **rooftop restaurant, Le Tchanqué**. The restaurant serves local seafood and French cuisine in a stylish, laid-back atmosphere. The hotel's location makes it easy to explore the **Cité du Vin**, **Jardin Public**, and **Bassin des Lumières**.

Amenities include:

- **Rooftop restaurant** with panoramic views

- **Fitness center**

- **Pet-friendly accommodations**

- **Bicycle rentals** for exploring the nearby quays

Hotel Indigo Bordeaux is ideal for travelers who want to experience the artistic and cultural side of Bordeaux while staying in a vibrant neighborhood.

Hotel Konti

Location: 10 Rue Montesquieu, 33000 Bordeaux, France

Phone: +33 5 56 52 60 60

Website: hotelkonti.com

Price Range: From €160 per night

Hotel Konti, located near **Place Gambetta**, is a trendy art deco hotel that provides a mix of modern comfort and historical elegance. The hotel offers 51 rooms with chic decor, blending modern amenities with the charm of Bordeaux's architectural history. The **bar and lounge** area is a great place to unwind with a drink, while the central location puts you within walking distance of Bordeaux's main attractions, including the **Place de la Bourse** and **Rue Sainte-Catherine**.

Amenities include:

- **Art Deco design** and stylish rooms

- **Bar and lounge** for casual relaxation

- **Business center**

- **Concierge services** for dining and sightseeing recommendations

Hotel Konti is perfect for travelers seeking a mix of historic charm and contemporary amenities in a prime location.

Budget-Friendly Stays:

B&B Hôtel Bordeaux Centre Gare Saint-Jean

Location: 126 Rue Emile Zola, 33800
Bordeaux, France
Phone: +33 8 92 78 81 06
Website: hotel-bb.com

Price Range: From €65 per night

Conveniently located near Bordeaux's main train station, **B&B Hôtel Bordeaux Centre Gare Saint-Jean** offers travelers affordable and comfortable accommodation. This hotel is ideal for budget-conscious tourists who still want easy access to Bordeaux's attractions. Rooms are simple but equipped with the essentials: air conditioning, flat-screen TVs, and free Wi-Fi. The location is perfect for those planning day trips by train or bus, as well as exploring the nearby Saint-Michel district, known for its markets and vibrant atmosphere.

Amenities include:

- **Free Wi-Fi**

- **Buffet breakfast**

- **24-hour reception**

- **Air-conditioned rooms**

- **Paid parking** nearby

This hotel is a great option for solo travelers, couples, or families looking for a no-frills stay close to transport links.

ibis Bordeaux Centre Bastide

Location: 16 Allée Serr, 33100 Bordeaux, France

Phone: +33 5 57 30 00 90

Website: ibis.accor.com

Price Range: From €70 per night

Located across the Garonne River in the quiet Bastide district, **ibis Bordeaux Centre Bastide** provides affordable, clean accommodations while keeping you close to the city's heart. The hotel is a short tram ride or a pleasant 15-minute walk from the city center. Rooms are cozy, modern, and well-maintained, offering everything you need for a comfortable stay without breaking the bank.

Amenities include:

- **Free Wi-Fi**

- **On-site bar**

- **Breakfast buffet**

- **Pet-friendly** rooms

- **24-hour front desk**

Perfect for travelers who prefer a quieter location but still want to be close to the action, ibis Bordeaux Centre Bastide delivers both comfort and value.

Hôtel Stars Bordeaux Gare

Location: 34 Rue de Tauzia, 33800 Bordeaux, France
Phone: +33 5 56 94 59 00
Website: stars-bordeaux-gare.com

Price Range: From €55 per night

Hôtel Stars Bordeaux Gare is another budget-friendly option near Bordeaux's Gare Saint-Jean, perfect for tourists looking for basic, clean accommodations close to transport hubs. The hotel offers simple, functional rooms with en-suite bathrooms and satellite TV. While the décor is modest, the affordable pricing and convenient location make it a great choice for budget-conscious travelers, especially those passing through on short stays.

Amenities include:

- **Free Wi-Fi** in public areas

- **Continental breakfast**

- **Bar**

- **24-hour reception**

- **Nearby public parking**

This hotel is a good fit for those seeking a basic, cost-effective option near Bordeaux's train station.

Hostel 20

Location: 20 Rue Borie, 33300 Bordeaux, France

Phone: +33 5 56 23 94 94

Website: hostel20bordeaux.com

Price Range: From €30 per night (dormitory); €50 per night (private rooms)

Located in the lively Chartrons district.

Hostel 20 offers a social, communal environment perfect for backpackers and solo travelers. The hostel has both dormitory beds and private rooms, providing flexibility for different types of travelers. The cozy common areas make it easy to meet fellow guests, and the hostel's location puts you near popular local attractions like the Cité du Vin and Bordeaux's waterfront.

Amenities include:

- **Free Wi-Fi**

- **Shared kitchen**

- **Lounge areas**

- **Luggage storage**

- **24-hour front desk**

With its friendly atmosphere and budget pricing, Hostel 20 is a fantastic choice for those who enjoy social stays while exploring Bordeaux.

Première Classe Bordeaux Nord-Lac

Location: Rue du Professeur Georges Jeanneney, 33300 Bordeaux, France

Phone: +33 5 56 39 31 24

Website: premiereclasse.com

Price Range: From €45 per night

Situated near Bordeaux Lac, **Première Classe Bordeaux Nord-Lac** offers affordable accommodations for travelers who don't mind staying slightly outside the city center. The hotel is accessible via tram, making it easy to reach the city's main attractions while enjoying the peace and quiet of the Bordeaux Lac area. Rooms are compact but functional, equipped with basic amenities for a comfortable stay.

Amenities include:

- **Free Wi-Fi**

- **Free parking**

- **Breakfast buffet**

- **Air-conditioned rooms**

- **24-hour reception**

This no-frills hotel is a great option for those seeking low-cost lodging with easy access to both Bordeaux's shopping district and the serene Bordeaux Lac.

A

lternative Accommodations: Apartments, guesthouses, and Airbnb options:

Appart'hôtel Victoria Garden Bordeaux

Location: 127 Cours de la Somme, 33800 Bordeaux, France

Phone: +33 5 56 33 48 48

Website: victoriagarden.com

Price Range: From €90 per night

Appart'hôtel Victoria Garden Bordeaux offers apartment-style accommodations, making it an ideal option for long-term travelers or families looking for a more independent stay. Each apartment is equipped with a **kitchenette**, allowing guests to prepare their meals. The hotel is located near Bordeaux's main public transport, providing easy access to the city center and other attractions.

Amenities include:

- **Spacious apartments** ranging from studios to two-room units

- **Private parking**

- **Free Wi-Fi**

- **Breakfast buffet**

- **Self-service laundry facilities**

This accommodation is perfect for travelers who prefer the comforts of home during their stay in Bordeaux, particularly those on longer visits who need practical amenities.

Mama Shelter Bordeaux

Location: 19 Rue Poquelin Molière, 33000 Bordeaux, France

Phone: +33 5 57 30 45 45

Website: mamashelter.com

Price Range: From €130 per night

Mama Shelter Bordeaux is a quirky and stylish option located in the heart of the city. This popular accommodation offers a mix of hotel rooms and apartment-style stays, making it great for both short and long-term visitors. The hotel is known for its vibrant rooftop bar, where guests can enjoy a drink while taking in panoramic views of Bordeaux.

Amenities include:

- **Rooftop restaurant and bar**

- **Free Wi-Fi**

- **Cinema and entertainment spaces**

- **Pet-friendly policies**

- **In-room kitchenettes** (in selected apartments)

Mama Shelter's funky design and lively atmosphere make it perfect for younger travelers or those looking for a unique, trendy experience in the center of Bordeaux.

Séjours & Affaires Bordeaux de L'Yser

Location: 183 Cours de l'Yser, 33800 Bordeaux, France

Phone: +33 5 57 97 01 01

Website: sejours-affaires.com

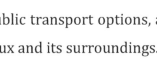

Price Range: From €75 per night

Séjours & Affaires Bordeaux de L'Yser provides budget-friendly apartment accommodations with convenient kitchenettes, perfect for those who prefer to cook their meals during their stay. The location is close to public transport options, allowing guests to easily explore Bordeaux and its surroundings.

Amenities include:

- **Kitchenettes** in each unit

- **Laundry facilities**

- **Free Wi-Fi**

- **Private parking**

- **Weekly housekeeping service**

This accommodation is ideal for budget-conscious travelers who still want the convenience of an apartment during their stay.

Family-Friendly Hotels

Novotel Bordeaux Lac

Location: Avenue Jean Gabriel Domergue, 33300 Bordeaux, France

Phone: +33 5 56 43 65 00

Website: novotel.com

Price Range: From €110 per night

Novotel Bordeaux Lac is located by the serene lake of Bordeaux Lac, offering a perfect environment for families. This hotel features **family rooms** that accommodate up to four people, making it an ideal choice for travelers with children. Kids will love the **outdoor pool** and the dedicated **play area**, where they can enjoy games and activities in a safe and engaging environment. The hotel's restaurant offers a kid-friendly menu, while the surrounding area provides opportunities for family-friendly outdoor activities such as biking and walking along the lakeside.

Other amenities include:

- **Free parking**

- **Fitness center**

- **Room service**

- **Pet-friendly rooms** (on request)

- **Nearby tram stop** for easy access to Bordeaux city center

Novotel Bordeaux Lac is a great choice for families seeking both relaxation and convenient access to Bordeaux's attractions.

Hôtel Mercure Bordeaux Lac

Location: Rue du Grand Barail, Quartier du Lac, 33300 Bordeaux, France

Phone: +33 5 56 43 36 72

Website: mercure.accor.com

Price Range: From €130 per night

Hôtel Mercure Bordeaux Lac is another excellent family-friendly option near Bordeaux's Lake district. This 4-star hotel offers **spacious family rooms** with modern amenities, perfect for families looking for both comfort and style.

The hotel has an **outdoor pool**, and its location near Bordeaux Lac makes it easy to engage in water-based activities or explore the local shops and restaurants.

Other amenities include:

- **Free Wi-Fi**

- **On-site restaurant** with kid-friendly options

- **Fitness facilities**

- **Free parking**

The Mercure Bordeaux Lac is ideal for families looking to balance a relaxing lakeside retreat with proximity to the city's bustling attractions.

Hôtel Vatel Bordeaux

Location: 4 Cours du Médoc, 33300 Bordeaux, France

Phone: +33 5 56 01 01 00

Website: hotelvatel.com

Price Range: From €150 per night

Located near the riverfront, **Hôtel Vatel Bordeaux** offers **spacious rooms and suites** tailored for families. The hotel is well-known for its focus on hospitality, with **concierge services** available to help plan family outings or recommend child-friendly restaurants and attractions. The hotel's proximity to the Garonne River allows easy access to riverfront activities and the nearby **Cité du Vin** Museum.

Amenities include:

- **In-room dining services**

- **Laundry services**

- **Private parking**

- **On-site restaurant** with family meal options

This hotel is perfect for families who want to experience Bordeaux's cultural highlights while enjoying comfortable and spacious accommodations.

Radisson Blu Hotel Bordeaux

Location: 63 Rue Lucien Faure, Bassins à Flot, 33300 Bordeaux, France
Phone: +33 5 56 01 29 00
Website: radissonhotels.com

Price Range: From €160 per night

Located in the trendy Bassins à Flot district, **Radisson Blu Hotel Bordeaux** is a family-friendly haven, offering **large rooms with river views**. The hotel's relaxed atmosphere and welcoming staff make it ideal for families visiting Bordeaux. There's a **fitness center**, but the highlight for families is the **family rooms** equipped with all the necessary amenities to ensure a comfortable stay. The hotel is also close to the **La Cité du Vin** Museum and the Bassins à Flot, where families can enjoy waterfront walks and dining.

Amenities include:

- **Free Wi-Fi**

- **On-site dining** with kid-friendly menu options

- **Room service**

- **Pet-friendly accommodations**

Radisson Blu is perfect for families who want to stay in a vibrant, modern area of Bordeaux while still enjoying plenty of family-friendly comforts.

All Suites Appart Hôtel Bordeaux Lac

Location: Rue du Professeur Georges Jeanneney, 33300 Bordeaux, France

Phone: +33 5 56 50 55 55

Website: all-suites.com

Price Range: From €80 per night

For families on a budget, **All Suites Appart Hôtel Bordeaux Lac** offers **apartment-style accommodations** with fully equipped kitchens, making it easy to prepare meals for picky eaters or enjoy a quiet dinner in. The hotel is located near Bordeaux Lac, providing easy access to outdoor activities and family-friendly attractions. Each suite is spacious, and the hotel offers flexible stays, from short-term visits to longer family vacations.

Amenities include:

- **Free parking**

- **Fitness center**

- **Laundry facilities**

- **Pet-friendly suites**

This hotel is a great option for families seeking a budget-friendly, flexible stay without sacrificing comfort

CHAPTER 10: PRACTICAL TRAVEL TIPS

Getting Around Bordeaux: Trams, Buses, and Bicycles

Bordeaux's public transportation system, **TBM (Transports Bordeaux Métropole)**, offers an efficient way to explore the city and its surroundings. Whether you prefer trams, buses, or bicycles, getting around is convenient and affordable.

Trams

Bordeaux's tram network consists of four lines (A, B, C, and D), covering key areas of the city. Trams run from 5:00 AM to midnight on weekdays, with extended hours until 1:00 AM on weekends. Trams are a reliable way to visit popular attractions, such as **La Cité du Vin** and **Place de la Bourse**.

Tickets cost **€1.90** for a single trip (valid for one hour), or you can buy a **10-trip ticket for €14.50**, ideal if you're staying longer.

Buses

The bus network complements the tram system, providing access to areas not served by trams. Buses operate from early morning until late evening, with frequent services throughout the day. A popular option is the **evening pass for €3**, which offers unlimited travel from 7:00 PM to 5:00 AM, perfect if you're planning to explore Bordeaux's nightlife. Buses are easy to use, but remember to wave them down as they approach your stop.

Bicycles

Bordeaux is a bike-friendly city, and the **V3 bike-sharing service** makes it easy to rent a bike and explore at your own pace. With **200 docking stations** across the city, it's convenient to pick up and drop off bikes. The first 30 minutes are free, and after that, it costs **€2 per hour**. For visitors, a **7-day pass** costs **€12**, offering flexibility for longer stays.

You can purchase transport tickets at tram stops, onboard buses, or via the **TBM app**, which allows mobile ticketing.

Bordeaux's comprehensive transportation system ensures you can easily explore everything this beautiful city has to offer.

Currency and Money Matters

When visiting Bordeaux, the currency used is the **Euro (€)**, which is divided into 100 cents. Bills come in denominations of €5, €10, €20, €50, and higher, while coins range from 1 cent to €2. Most businesses accept credit and debit cards, but it's still a good idea to carry some cash, especially for smaller establishments, markets, or transportation in rural areas.

Currency Exchange: You can exchange money at banks, post offices, or specialized currency exchange offices across Bordeaux. While exchange services are available at Bordeaux–Mérignac Airport, the rates tend to be higher, so it's better to exchange money in the city. Avoid exchanging currency at airports as the fees can be significantly marked up. Instead, consider ordering travel money online through services that offer competitive rates or using **travel cards** like Wise to avoid costly conversion rates.

ATMs (Distributeurs Automatiques de Billets): ATMs are plentiful in Bordeaux and can be found at airports, train stations, and around the city center. They generally accept major cards like **Visa** and **Mastercard**. Be sure to always withdraw in **Euros** when given the option at the ATM, as selecting your home currency can lead to unfavorable exchange rates. Keep in mind that some ATMs may charge fees for withdrawals, so check with your bank beforehand.

Credit Cards and Payments: Credit cards are widely accepted, especially in urban areas. **Contactless payments** have become more common post-pandemic, but it's always a good idea to carry small amounts of cash for smaller vendors or tips. **American Express** may not be accepted everywhere, so Visa and Mastercard are more reliable.

Budgeting Tips: Expect to spend around €10-15 for a simple lunch, €20-35 for a casual dinner, and €3-6 for a glass of local wine. Public transport, such as trams, is budget-friendly, with day passes costing around €5-10. Entrance fees for major attractions like museums typically range from €7-20.

By planning and keeping an eye on exchange rates, you can avoid unnecessary fees and make your money go further while enjoying everything Bordeaux has to offer.

Language and Communication: Basic French Phrases

When traveling to Bordeaux, a little French goes a long way in enhancing your experience. While many locals, especially in tourist areas, speak some English, knowing basic French phrases will not only help you communicate but also earn you more welcoming responses from the French, who appreciate the effort.

Here are 20 essential French phrases that will be helpful during your stay, especially for dining, transport, and general communication:

1. **Bonjour** – Hello

2. **Merci beaucoup** – Thank you very much

3. **S'il vous plaît** – Please

4. **Excusez-moi** – Excuse me

5. **Où est...?** – Where is...? (e.g., Où est la gare? – Where is the train station?)

6. **Je voudrais...** – I would like... (useful in restaurants)

7. **L'addition, s'il vous plaît** – The bill, please

8. **Combien ça coûte?** – How much does it cost?

9. **Je ne comprends pas** – I don't understand

10. **Pouvez-vous répéter, s'il vous plaît?** – Could you repeat, please?

11. **Parlez-vous anglais?** – Do you speak English?

12. **Où sont les toilettes?** – Where are the restrooms?

13. **Comment allez-vous?** – How are you? (polite)

14. **Ça va?** – How are you? (informal)

15. **Je suis allergique à...** – I am allergic to... (useful for food allergies, e.g., les produits laitiers for dairy)

16. **Le menu, s'il vous plaît** – The menu, please

17. **À quelle heure est...?** – What time is...? (e.g., À quelle heure est le musée ouvert? – What time is the museum open?)

18. **Est-ce que je peux payer avec une carte de crédit?** – Can I pay with a credit card?

19. **Pardon** – Sorry (useful for small apologies in crowded places)

20. **Je cherche...** – I'm looking for... (e.g., Je cherche un taxi – I'm looking for a taxi)

For non-French speakers, it's advisable to start every interaction with a polite "Bonjour" and try to use French as much as possible before switching to English. French people tend to appreciate politeness and a genuine effort to speak their language. Using translation apps like Google Translate or language apps like Duolingo can also be handy for improving your communication during your trip.

Mobile Apps for Travelers in Bordeaux

When traveling to Bordeaux, several mobile apps can make your trip smoother and more enjoyable. Here are some essential ones to consider for 2024:

1. **Bordeaux City Pass**: This app is a must for exploring Bordeaux. It offers discounts and free access to top attractions, along with public transport information.

2. **Google Maps**: Essential for navigation, it provides accurate public transport details, walking routes, and directions to landmarks.

3. **LaFourchette**: Use this app to reserve tables at Bordeaux's best restaurants and even score discounts.

4. **Google Translate**: Handy for translating French menus or signs with the photo-translate feature.

5. **Vivino**: If you're a wine lover, this app lets you scan wine labels, access tasting notes, and track wines you've enjoyed during your Bordeaux trip.

Understanding French Tipping Etiquette

Tipping in Bordeaux, as in the rest of France, differs significantly from countries like the United States. In French restaurants, cafés, and bars, the **service charge (15%) is always included** in the bill. You'll often see this noted as "service comprise" on the menu or receipt. However, while tipping is not required, it is common to leave **a small tip** as a gesture of appreciation for good service.

For restaurants, if you've had great service, it's customary to leave **€1 to €2 per person** for casual dining or **5-10%** of the bill in more upscale restaurants. In cafés, it's typical to round up your bill or leave **50 centimes to €1** for a coffee or drink. Keep in mind that large tips are considered unnecessary and can sometimes be seen as excessive in France.

Tipping in Hotels

When staying at a hotel, tipping depends on the level of service. For porters who help with luggage, it's customary to tip **€1-2 per bag**. If a concierge assists with special requests, like making restaurant reservations or booking tours, tipping **€5-10** is a kind gesture. Similarly, housekeepers are usually tipped **€1-2 per day** for keeping the room tidy.

Tipping for Taxis and Rideshares

Taxi drivers in Bordeaux do not expect tips, but it is polite to round up the fare to the nearest euro. For longer trips or when the driver helps with luggage, you can offer a tip of **5-10%** of the fare. For ride-sharing services like Uber, tips are optional and can be added through the app.

Remember, tipping in France is more about showing appreciation for good service rather than an obligation. Carrying small change is useful as most tips are left in cash

CHAPTER 11: SEASONAL EVENTS AND FESTIVALS

Bordeaux Wine Festival (Fête le Vin):

The **Bordeaux Wine Festival** is one of the city's most iconic events, attracting thousands of wine lovers from around the world. Held annually along the scenic quays of Bordeaux, the festival is set for **June 19-22, 2025**. This four-day celebration showcases the rich wine heritage of Bordeaux, allowing visitors to taste a variety of wines from the region's **80 appellations**. The **Tasting Pass**, which can be purchased in advance, gives you access to wine tastings and workshops with local experts, providing an immersive experience into Bordeaux's viticulture.

The event also features **tall ships** moored along the Garonne River, a nod to the city's maritime history. Visitors can tour these historic vessels, adding a unique touch to the wine-tasting experience. One of the highlights of the festival is the **drone light show**, which illuminates the skies over the river, creating a breathtaking spectacle.

For wine enthusiasts or a curious traveler, the festival offers something for everyone. Be sure to visit the **gastronomy village** where you can enjoy local food pairings with your wine, including cheeses and charcuterie from the region. If you're traveling with family, don't miss the **Anima'Vigne workshops** that engage both kids and adults in fun, wine-themed games.

The Bordeaux River Festival:

Celebrating the city's deep connection to the Garonne River, the **Bordeaux River Festival** brings maritime culture to life every other year. Scheduled for **May 2025**, this festival transforms the quays into a vibrant maritime village with activities, performances, and exhibits dedicated to Bordeaux's nautical heritage. The highlight of the festival is the impressive fleet of **tall ships** that sail into the city, offering visitors the chance to explore these historic vessels.

The riverfront is buzzing with live music, street performances, and craft stalls, ensuring there's something for everyone. If you're into water sports, the river festival offers opportunities for **kayaking** and **boat races**, making it a great choice for those seeking a more active experience. There are also **fireworks** displays over the Garonne, adding an extra layer of magic to the evenings.

For a more relaxed experience, head to one of the many food stalls along the waterfront, offering local delicacies and Bordeaux wines. Families will also find plenty of kid-friendly activities, such as maritime-themed games and workshops.

Les Epicuriales: Gastronomy Festival:

For foodies visiting Bordeaux, the **Les Epicuriales** festival is a must-see. Taking place annually from **late May to early June**, this gastronomic event transforms the **Allées de Tourny** into an open-air gourmet village. Renowned local chefs and restaurants set up pop-up kitchens, offering visitors a chance to taste dishes from **Bordeaux's best eateries**.

The event is not just about food; it's a full gastronomic experience, featuring cooking workshops, live demonstrations, and wine pairings that showcase the region's culinary talents. You can sample everything from traditional French cuisine to innovative fusion dishes, all in a lively, social atmosphere.

A popular part of the festival is the **Epicuriales Bar**, where you can relax with a glass of Bordeaux wine or a crafted cocktail while enjoying live music performances. Make sure to book your tickets early for the chef's **"dinner under the stars"**—an exclusive evening dining experience where top chefs prepare multi-course meals right on the Allées.

The Bordeaux International Independent Film Festival:

A true treat for cinema lovers, the **Bordeaux International Independent Film Festival** (Festival International du Film Indépendant de Bordeaux) showcases the very best of independent cinema. Held in **October 2025**, the festival presents a diverse lineup of films from around the world, spanning genres from experimental shorts to full-length features.

What makes this festival special is its focus on emerging filmmakers, giving a platform to up-and-coming talent. Screenings take place across various venues in the city, including the **UGC Cinema** and the **Cinéma Utopia**, where you can catch films in intimate settings followed by Q&A sessions with the filmmakers themselves.

Besides film screenings, the festival includes **workshops** on filmmaking, discussions on the future of independent cinema, and networking events for industry professionals. It's a fantastic opportunity for travelers who love film and are keen to experience the vibrant creative scene of Bordeaux.

Christmas Markets and Winter Festivals:

The holiday season in Bordeaux comes alive with festive spirit, starting in **late November** and running through **December 2025**. The city's Christmas Market, located in **Place des Quinconces**, is one of the largest in the region, offering over 150 wooden chalets selling handmade crafts, artisanal foods, and holiday gifts.

Stroll through the market with a cup of **vin chaud** (mulled wine) while listening to Christmas carols or watch as children marvel at the **giant Christmas tree** in the center of the square. Food lovers will enjoy the **regional specialties** on offer, including roasted chestnuts, gingerbread, and savory tartiflette.

The market, Bordeaux also hosts **ice-skating rinks**, holiday-themed performances, and **light shows** projected onto historic buildings. One of the key highlights is the **Fête des Lumières** (Festival of Lights), which illuminates the city in spectacular light displays, making a winter visit to Bordeaux truly magical.

CHAPTER 12: LOCAL LAWS AND CUSTOMS

Essential French Laws for Tourists

When visiting Bordeaux, there are some essential French laws you need to be aware of to ensure a smooth and enjoyable trip. One of the key requirements is that you **must always carry identification**. For tourists, this means your passport or a copy of it. If you're driving in France, you should also have your driver's license, vehicle registration, and proof of insurance on hand. Failing to present these documents upon request could result in fines up to €38, and in more severe cases, even higher penalties.

If you're renting a car, note that **France drives on the right**, and **seatbelts are mandatory** for all passengers. Children under 10 must sit in an appropriate child safety seat or booster, and mobile phone use while driving is strictly prohibited, even with hands-free systems. In 2024, France introduced **digital driving licenses** for residents, which tourists from abroad will not be able to use, so keep a physical copy of your license. Driving without proper documentation or using unauthorized devices to detect speed cameras can result in steep fines or even the impoundment of your vehicle.

If you're exploring Bordeaux by foot, be aware that **jaywalking laws** are enforced, and pedestrians should always cross at designated areas. Lastly, it's illegal to cover your face in public spaces, such as wearing full-face masks outside of holidays or events like Carnival. Respecting these laws will help you avoid any unnecessary trouble during your stay.

How to Behave Respectfully in Bordeaux

Bordeaux is known for its warm hospitality, but as a tourist, there are some customs and behaviors to keep in mind to show respect for local culture. **Greetings** in France are particularly important. A polite "Bonjour" (good morning) or "Bonsoir" (good evening) when entering shops, restaurants, or even elevators is expected. Failing to greet someone can come across as rude. In more formal settings, shaking hands is the norm, and in casual settings, locals often greet each other with a light kiss on the cheek, known as "la bise."

When dining out, remember that **tipping** is not as customary in France as in some other countries. A service charge is usually included in the bill, but leaving a small amount (about 5-10%) is appreciated if the service was particularly good. Also, avoid raising your voice in public or speaking too loudly in restaurants, as this is considered impolite.

The dress code in Bordeaux is generally smart-casual. Locals tend to dress stylishly, especially when dining out, so wearing neat, well-put-together outfits can help you blend in. In religious or historic sites, modest clothing is required, and showing excessive skin can be seen as disrespectful.

Finally, **littering** and disrespecting public spaces are frowned upon. Bordeaux takes pride in its cleanliness, so always dispose of your trash properly and respect the environment.

Alcohol, Smoking, and Legal Drinking Ages

In France, the **legal drinking age** is 18 for all alcoholic beverages. It's common to see locals enjoying a glass of wine with meals, but it's important to know that **public drunkenness** is not well-tolerated, and fines may be imposed if you're visibly intoxicated in public spaces. Openly consuming alcohol in public, outside of designated places like bars and restaurants, is also prohibited in many areas, including popular tourist spots.

Smoking laws are quite strict. **Smoking indoors** in public places, including restaurants, bars, and cafes, has been banned since 2007. Most establishments offer outdoor seating where smoking is allowed, and you'll often see designated smoking areas in public places. In 2024, laws around **vaping** have become more aligned with traditional smoking, with restrictions on indoor use and a general push for designated outdoor areas.

You'll find that **wine and tobacco** are deeply intertwined in French culture, but always be mindful of where and when you indulge. Stick to designated smoking areas and avoid excessive drinking in public to respect local customs and laws.

Opening Hours for Shops and Businesses

When it comes to opening hours in Bordeaux, most shops, including boutiques and supermarkets, open **around 9 or 10 AM** and close by **7 or 8 PM**. However, unlike in some countries, **many smaller shops close for a midday break**, particularly in quieter neighborhoods. This "sieste" period often falls between 12:30 PM and 2:30 PM, so it's good to plan around it, especially if you're visiting smaller family-owned businesses.

On **Sundays**, many shops and supermarkets are closed, though some larger supermarkets and chain stores in tourist areas may remain open in the morning. Restaurants and cafes generally stay open later, especially in tourist-friendly areas like the **Quinconces and Chartrons** districts, where restaurants are open until **10 or 11 PM**.

Business hours can vary significantly during holidays and special events, such as Christmas or Bastille Day. Many stores and public offices will either be closed or operate on limited hours during these times. In December, Bordeaux's **Christmas markets** extend their hours, staying open late into the evening, adding to the festive spirit.

CHAPTER 13: ESSENTIALS FOR EVERY TRAVELER

What to Pack for a Trip to Bordeaux

Packing for Bordeaux depends heavily on the season and the activities you plan. Here are some essentials to make your trip comfortable, stylish, and practical:

Spring (March-May): Bordeaux in spring can be mild but with occasional rain. Bring **light layers**, like a jacket, sweater, and long-sleeve shirts. A **compact umbrella** or a **light raincoat** will be handy. Don't forget **comfortable walking shoes** the cobbled streets of Bordeaux can be tough on your feet.

Summer (June-August): Summer temperatures can rise, so pack **breathable fabrics** like cotton or linen. You'll need **sunscreen**, **sunglasses**, and a **hat** to protect against the sun, especially if you plan to spend time at vineyards or outdoor markets. For evening dinners at a nice restaurant, pack a **dressier outfit** think light dresses, or a smart-casual ensemble with comfortable shoes. If you plan to head to nearby beaches, don't forget a **swimsuit**.

Fall (September-November): Bordeaux in the fall can be unpredictable, with cooler temperatures in the morning and evening, but warmer afternoons. Bring **layers**, such as a jacket and scarve, and **closed shoes**. A light rain jacket is also a good idea, as showers are more common this time of year.

Winter (December-February): Winters are mild but wet. You'll need a **warm coat**, **waterproof shoes**, and a **hat** to stay cozy while exploring. Pack a good **pair of boots** that can handle both city streets and countryside mud if you're visiting vineyards.

Special Items: If you're planning a wine tour, pack a **small bag** to carry bottles or purchases. For day trips to the countryside, **hiking shoes** and a **light backpack** will be useful. Lastly, a **universal adapter** for charging your devices is essential for non-European travelers.

By planning your wardrobe around the season and activities, you'll be able to enjoy Bordeaux comfortably and stylishly.

How to Stay Safe in Bordeaux

Bordeaux is generally a safe city, but like any destination, it's important to stay vigilant. Here are some practical tips for staying safe:

Avoiding Scams: In tourist-heavy areas like Place de la Bourse and the shopping streets, be aware of common tourist scams.

These may include people asking for signatures for fake petitions or offering "free" bracelets, only to demand money afterward. Politely decline and move on.

Crowded Areas: Pickpockets can operate in crowded places such as public transport, markets, and festivals. Use a **money belt** or a **secure bag** with a zipper. Avoid keeping valuable items in easily accessible pockets. In places like Saint-André Cathedral or Marché des Capucins, stay aware of your surroundings, especially when snapping photos or using your phone.

Nighttime Safety: Bordeaux is lively at night, especially in areas like Saint Pierre and near the Garonne River. Stick to well-lit, busy streets if you're out late. The student area near Place de la Victoire can be loud but usually safe. Take extra care in more secluded areas late at night.

Emergency Contacts: In case of emergencies, dial **112** for general emergencies or **17** for the police. If you encounter any safety concerns, don't hesitate to contact local authorities or hotel staff for assistance.

Local Laws: Respect Bordeaux's public drinking laws. While it's common to enjoy a bottle of wine at a picnic, open drinking in non-designated public areas can result in fines.

By following these tips, you'll ensure a smooth and safe visit to Bordeaux.

Traveling with Kids in Bordeaux

Bordeaux is a family-friendly city with plenty to offer for both children and parents. Here are some tips to make your family trip enjoyable:

Kid-Friendly Attractions: Bordeaux offers several parks like **Jardin Public**, where children can enjoy the playgrounds and parents can relax by the ponds. For a fun learning experience, take your kids to **Cap Sciences**, an interactive museum that explores science and technology. Another must-visit is the **Zoo de Bordeaux-Pessac**, perfect for a family day out.

Wine Tours with Kids: While Bordeaux is famous for its wine, many vineyards and châteaux also offer activities to keep children entertained, like **Château d'Agassac**, which has a treasure hunt designed for kids while adults enjoy wine tastings. Consider booking a family-friendly vineyard tour where kids can participate in other activities like garden tours or meeting farm animals.

Child-Friendly Dining: Many restaurants in Bordeaux offer kids' menus, especially in family-friendly neighborhoods like **Chartrons**. Head to **Marché des Capucins** for a casual family meal, where you can sample local food and let the kids enjoy the lively atmosphere.

Getting Around with Kids: Bordeaux's **tram system** is stroller-friendly, and **buses** are equipped to accommodate families with young children. If you're exploring the city center, many pedestrianized areas make it easy to stroll with a buggy. Consider renting bikes from one of the city's **V3 bike stations**, as some have child seats attached.

With Bordeaux's parks, museums, and family-oriented activities, traveling with kids here can be a memorable experience for all ages.

Accessibility and Mobility in the City

Bordeaux has made significant strides in ensuring accessibility for travelers with mobility challenges. Here's what you need to know for a smooth experience:

Public Transport: Bordeaux's **tram system** is one of the most accessible in France. Trams are equipped with low floors, making it easy for travelers using wheelchairs to board. Most buses are also accessible, with ramps and designated spaces for wheelchairs. For a stress-free trip, use the **TBM Bordeaux transport app**, which provides real-time information about accessible services and routes.

Wheelchair-Friendly Attractions: Many of Bordeaux's top attractions, including the **Cité du Vin**, **Musée d'Aquitaine**, and the **Jardin Public**, offer accessible entrances and facilities. Historic sites like **Place de la Bourse** are mostly accessible, though cobblestone streets may present some challenges, so consider bringing a sturdy wheelchair or mobility scooter.

Accessible Accommodation: Numerous hotels, such as **Radisson Blu Bordeaux** and **Novotel Bordeaux Centre**, offer accessible rooms with roll-in showers and wider doorways. Always confirm accessibility features when booking to ensure a smooth stay.

Navigating Cobblestone Streets: Bordeaux's historic center has many cobblestone streets, which can be tricky to navigate for those with mobility issues. It's a good idea to wear comfortable shoes and consider renting a **mobility scooter** for longer distances. For travelers using wheelchairs, it's advisable to plan routes, using accessible pathways where possible.

Bordeaux's commitment to accessibility ensures that travelers with special mobility needs can explore the city comfortably and enjoy all it has to offer.

CHAPTER 14: 3-DAY, 5-DAY, AND 7-DAY ITINERARIES

3-Day Itinerary: Bordeaux Highlights

Day 1: Explore the Historic Center of Bordeaux

Morning

Start your trip with a visit to **Place de la Bourse**, one of Bordeaux's most iconic squares. Directly in front of it, you'll find the **Miroir d'Eau**, the world's largest reflecting pool, where you can capture stunning photos of the city's architecture mirrored in the water. Afterward, head to **Saint-André Cathedral**, a UNESCO World Heritage site dating back to the 12th century. Its impressive Gothic style and the **Pey Berland Tower** offer panoramic views of the city from above

Afternoon

Enjoy lunch at **Le Petit Commerce**, a seafood bistro offering a range of fresh local dishes. Afterward, stroll down **Rue Sainte-

Catherine, Europe's longest pedestrian shopping street, filled with boutiques and cafes. Take time to visit **Porte Cailhau**, a 15th-century gate that offers great views of the Garonne River

Evening

For dinner, book a table at **Le 7 Restaurant**, located on the top floor of **La Cité du Vin**. This restaurant not only offers excellent regional cuisine but also provides a panoramic view of Bordeaux's skyline. End your evening with a **Garonne River Cruise**, where you can enjoy the illuminated cityscape while sipping local wine.

Day 2: Museums and Art

Morning

Start the day by visiting **Musée d'Aquitaine**, which showcases Bordeaux's history from prehistoric times through the Roman era to the modern day. Afterward, take a short walk to the **CAPC Musée d'Art Contemporain**, housed in a former warehouse, to view cutting-edge modern art exhibits.

Afternoon

For lunch, head to **Les Halles de Bacalan**, a lively food market where you can sample a variety of local produce and dishes. Spend the afternoon at **La Cité du Vin**, Bordeaux's unique wine museum. Explore its interactive exhibits about global wine culture and history, and finish with a wine tasting on the museum's 8th-floor terrace.

Evening

For a relaxed evening, take a stroll along the **Quais de Bordeaux**, the waterfront promenade, and enjoy dinner at **Le Gabriel**, a Michelin-starred restaurant at **Place de la Bourse**. Its elegant dining rooms and exceptional French cuisine make it a perfect place to end the day.

Day 3: Day Trip to Saint-Émilion

Morning

Spend your final day visiting the charming village of **Saint-Émilion**, located about 45 minutes from Bordeaux. Start with a tour of the **Monolithic Church**, carved directly into the limestone rock. Wander through the village's medieval streets, stopping to admire its ancient architecture.

Afternoon

Enjoy lunch at **L'Envers du Décor**, a cozy restaurant known for its local wine pairings. Spend the afternoon touring some of the region's most famous vineyards, such as **Château Troplong Mondot** or **Château Ausone**, both offering exceptional wine-tasting experiences.

Evening

Return to Bordeaux for a final dinner at **Brasserie Bordelaise**, a laid-back bistro specializing in traditional French cuisine, including perfectly cooked steak and local wines

5-Day Itinerary: Explore Bordeaux and Its Wine Regions

Day 1: Discover the Historic City of Bordeaux

Morning

Start your first day by exploring Bordeaux's historic center. Begin at the **Place de la Bourse** and the **Miroir d'Eau**, capturing the beautiful reflections of Bordeaux's classical architecture. Next, visit **Saint-André Cathedral** and climb the **Pey Berland Tower** for panoramic views of the city.

Afternoon

Enjoy lunch at **Le Petit Commerce**, a popular seafood bistro in the city center. After lunch, stroll down **Rue Sainte-Catherine**, the longest pedestrian shopping street in Europe. You can also visit **Porte Cailhau**, a medieval gate offering stunning views of the river.

Evening

For dinner, reserve a table at **Le 7 Restaurant** at **La Cité du Vin**, which not only offers exceptional food but also panoramic views of Bordeaux's skyline. Afterward, unwind with a **Garonne River Cruise**, where you can enjoy Bordeaux's illuminated landmarks

Day 2: Wine Tasting in Médoc

Morning

Head to the **Médoc wine region** for a day dedicated to wine tasting. Start at **Château Margaux**, one of Bordeaux's most prestigious estates. Learn about its history and indulge in tastings of their fine wines.

Afternoon

Continue your wine journey with a visit to **Château Pichon Longueville**, another top-tier winery. Enjoy a picnic lunch in the vineyards or a meal at a nearby restaurant like **La Table de Nathalie**, located within the vineyards. Spend the afternoon touring **Château Latour**, famous for its Grand Cru Classé wines.

Evening

Return to Bordeaux for a casual dinner at **Brasserie Bordelaise**, a restaurant known for its hearty French dishes and extensive selection of local wines.

Day 3: Explore Saint-Émilion

Morning

Take a day trip to the picturesque village of **Saint-Émilion**, a

UNESCO World Heritage site. Begin by exploring the **Monolithic Church**, an underground cathedral carved into limestone. Stroll through the charming medieval streets, visiting local shops and wine cellars.

Afternoon

Enjoy lunch at **L'Envers du Décor**, a cozy restaurant in the heart of the village, famous for its excellent wine pairings. Spend the afternoon touring some of Saint-Émilion's most famous wineries, such as **Château Troplong Mondot** or **Château Ausone**, where you can learn about their rich winemaking traditions.

Evening

Return to Bordeaux and enjoy a relaxing evening with dinner at **Le Gabriel**, located in **Place de la Bourse**. This Michelin-starred restaurant offers refined French cuisine with an elegant ambiance.

Day 4: Visit Arcachon and the Dune du Pilat

Morning

Spend the day on a coastal excursion to **Arcachon**, about an hour's drive from Bordeaux. Visit the **Dune du Pilat**, Europe's tallest sand dune, and climb to the top for breathtaking views of the Atlantic Ocean and surrounding pine forests.

Afternoon

Enjoy a seafood lunch at **Chez Pierre**, a waterfront restaurant in Arcachon, known for its fresh oysters. Afterward, take a boat tour of the **Bay of Arcachon**, where you can explore the **Île aux Oiseaux** and see its famous stilt houses.

Evening

Return to Bordeaux for a more relaxed evening with a casual dinner at **Madame Pang**, a dim sum bar offering a vibrant and fun atmosphere.

Day 5: Discover Pessac-Léognan and Sauternes

Morning

Start the day by visiting the **Pessac-Léognan** wine region. Begin with a tour and tasting at **Château Haut-Brion**, one of Bordeaux's top wineries known for both red and white wines. The estate offers fascinating insights into its winemaking process and history.

Afternoon

Head south to the **Sauternes** region, famous for its sweet dessert wines. Visit **Château d'Yquem**, one of the most prestigious wineries in the area. After a guided tour and wine tasting, enjoy lunch at a local vineyard restaurant

Evening

Return to Bordeaux and enjoy your final dinner at **Le Pressoir d'Argent Gordon Ramsay**, a two-Michelin-starred restaurant offering a memorable culinary experience. The menu is focused on using local ingredients, with perfectly paired Bordeaux wines.

7-Day Itinerary: Bordeaux, Vineyards, and Nearby Villages

Day 1: Arrival and Explore Central Bordeaux

Morning

Start your trip by exploring **Place de la Bourse** and the **Miroir d'Eau**, Bordeaux's famous reflecting pool. This area is iconic and offers great photo opportunities. Afterward, head to **Bordeaux Cathedral** (Saint-André) to admire its Gothic architecture and learn about the city's rich history.

Afternoon

Take a leisurely walk to the **Grand Théâtre de Bordeaux** and enjoy lunch at **Le Chien de Pavlov**, a local favorite serving French cuisine with a twist. In the afternoon, explore **Rue Sainte-Catherine**, Europe's longest pedestrian shopping street, filled with shops and cafes.

Evening

Enjoy a dinner cruise on the **Garonne River** to see Bordeaux's skyline illuminated at night. Many cruises include local wine tastings and a delicious meal

Day 2: Bordeaux's Museums and Art Scene

Morning

Visit **Musée d'Aquitaine**, where you can immerse yourself in Bordeaux's history from ancient times to modern-day. Then head to **CAPC Museum of Contemporary Art**, showcasing international modern art.

Afternoon

Have lunch at **Les Halles de Bacalan**, a food market offering a variety of local specialties. Afterward, visit **La Cité du Vin**, Bordeaux's famous wine museum, for interactive exhibits and a panoramic wine-tasting session.

Evening

End your day with dinner at **Le Gabriel**, a Michelin-starred restaurant located at Place de la Bourse, offering gourmet French cuisine.

Day 3: Day Trip to Saint-Émilion

Morning

Take a morning trip to **Saint-Émilion**, a UNESCO World Heritage village known for its wine. Start by visiting the **Monolithic Church**, carved into limestone, and wander through the town's medieval streets

Afternoon

Spend the afternoon touring local vineyards, such as **Château Troplong Mondot**, where you can enjoy tastings and learn about Saint-Émilion's prestigious wines. Have lunch at a local restaurant like **L'Envers du Décor**, known for its excellent wine pairings.

Evening

Return to Bordeaux and enjoy a quiet evening strolling along the **Quais de Bordeaux**, the waterfront promenade. Grab dinner at a casual bistro like **Le Petit Commerce**, known for its seafood.

Day 4: The Médoc Wine Route

Morning

Set out early for the **Médoc Wine Route**, starting at **Château Margaux**. This iconic vineyard offers guided tours of its vineyards and cellars, finishing with a tasting of its world-famous wines.

Afternoon

Continue to **Château Pichon Longueville**, another Grand Cru Classé, for a wine tour and picnic lunch in the vineyards. Explore the small village of **Pauillac** nearby, known for its wine estates.

Evening

Return to Bordeaux for dinner at **La Brasserie Bordelaise**, offering classic French dishes with a focus on local produce.

Day 5: Day Trip to Arcachon and the Dune du Pilat

Morning

Drive to **Arcachon** to visit the **Dune du Pilat**, Europe's tallest sand dune. Hike to the top for breathtaking views of the Atlantic Ocean and surrounding pine forests.

Afternoon

Have lunch in **Arcachon**, where you can enjoy fresh oysters at **Chez Pierre** on the seafront. Spend the afternoon exploring the **Bay of Arcachon**, either relaxing on the beach or taking a boat tour around the bay.

Evening

Return to Bordeaux in the evening and enjoy dinner at **Madame Pang**, a trendy dim sum bar offering a vibrant atmosphere.

Day 6: Graves and Sauternes Wine Regions

Morning

Begin your day with a visit to **Château de La Brède**, the former home of philosopher Montesquieu, located in the **Graves** wine region. Continue to **Château Haut-Brion**, a Premier Grand Cru Classé estate, for a tour and tasting.

Afternoon

Head to the **Sauternes** region, famous for its sweet wines. Tour **Château d'Yquem**, known for producing some of the world's finest dessert wines. Pair the tasting with a local lunch in the vineyards.

Evening

Return to Bordeaux for a final dinner at **Le Pressoir d'Argent Gordon Ramsay**, a two-star Michelin restaurant that offers an unforgettable culinary experience.

Day 7: Explore Bordeaux's Nearby Villages

Morning

Take a day trip to the nearby **Dordogne Valley**. Start with a visit to **Château de Beynac**, a medieval fortress overlooking the Dordogne River. Continue to **Sarlat-la-Canéda**, a beautiful medieval town known for its cobblestone streets and local markets.

Afternoon

Explore the prehistoric **Lascaux Caves**, famous for their ancient cave paintings. The nearby **Lascaux IV** replica offers an immersive experience that preserves the original art

Evening

Return to Bordeaux for your last night and enjoy a relaxed dinner at **Le 7 Restaurant**, located at the top of **La Cité du Vin** with panoramic views of the city.

CHAPTER 15: INSIDER TIPS FOR A WONDERFUL EXPERIENCE

Hidden Gems: Discovering the Lesser-Known Side of Bordeaux

Bordeaux may be famous for its wine and grand architecture, but it's also home to hidden gems that offer a deeper, more intimate connection with the city. Start your journey at **Place des Quinconces**, a vast square often overlooked by tourists. It's home to the Monument aux Girondins and is surrounded by lush green spaces—perfect for a peaceful stroll away from the city's hustle. Another treasure is the **Musée du Vin et du Négoce** in the Chartrons district. Unlike the more popular Cité du Vin, this museum delves into Bordeaux's wine trade history in a cozy, traditional setting, complete with tastings.

If you enjoy history, don't miss **Basilique Saint-Michel** in the Saint-Michel district. Its Gothic architecture and quiet atmosphere make it an excellent spot for reflection. For something truly off-the-beaten-path, visit **Darwin Ecosystem**, a former military barracks turned into an eco-friendly space filled with art, organic shops, and cultural events. This is a great place to explore Bordeaux's alternative side while soaking up creative energy.

Unique Experiences: Cooking Classes, Wine Workshops, and More

For a hands-on experience in Bordeaux, nothing beats learning from the locals. Enroll in a **cooking class** where you can master the art of French cuisine. One of the best places to do this is at **L'Atelier des Chefs**, where you'll learn to cook classic dishes like duck confit or canelés, Bordeaux's beloved caramelized pastries. These classes are intimate and led by expert chefs who teach you the secrets behind these iconic meals.

If wine is more your passion, Bordeaux offers numerous **wine workshops** that will elevate your appreciation of the region's famed wines. At **École du Vin**, you can attend workshops designed for beginners and enthusiasts alike, covering topics from grape varieties to food pairings. For a deeper connection to the terroir, visit the vineyards around Bordeaux for full-day tours and tastings, often paired with gourmet meals

Local Markets and Artisanal Boutiques

Exploring Bordeaux's local markets is a must for anyone who wants to immerse themselves in the city's culture. **Marché des Capucins**, Bordeaux's largest market, offers a vibrant array of fresh produce, seafood, and local delicacies. Open daily, this market is perfect for sampling local specialties like foie gras or stocking up on artisanal cheese and bread. For an even more local vibe, visit **Marché de Saint-Michel** on weekends, where you can find antiques and street food.

Artisanal boutiques are scattered throughout the city, especially in the **Saint-Pierre** and **Chartrons** districts. Look for **Cadiot-Badie**, a chocolate shop with over 200 years of history, or discover unique handmade goods at **Boutique Lalique**, which offers intricate crystal pieces.

Best Spots for Stunning Views of Bordeaux

For panoramic views of Bordeaux, head to **Pey Berland Tower**, adjacent to the Bordeaux Cathedral. Climbing to the top rewards you with an incredible vista of the city's historic rooftops and the Garonne River. Another favorite is the **Rooftop of La Cité**

du Vin, where you can enjoy a glass of wine while gazing at the cityscape.

For a more relaxed experience, visit the **Pont de Pierre** at sunset. This historic bridge offers stunning views of both banks of the Garonne, with the city glowing in the evening light. Alternatively, the **Public Garden** is perfect for those looking to enjoy Bordeaux's natural beauty while catching a glimpse of its architectural marvels.

CHAPTER 16: TRAVELER RESOURCES AND USEFUL CONTACTS

Tourist Information Centers

In Bordeaux, you'll find several tourist information centers that are invaluable for your trip. The main **Bordeaux Tourist Office**, located at **12 Cours du XXX Juillet**, is a hub of resources. Open from **9:00 AM to 6:30 PM** (with shorter hours on Sundays and holidays), it offers guided tours, city maps, brochures, and advice on must-see attractions. You can book tours of the vineyards, the UNESCO World Heritage sites, or even day trips around the region.

Another useful location is the **Gare Saint-Jean Information Center**, close to Bordeaux's main train station. This is perfect for travelers arriving by rail, providing essential services like hotel bookings, public transport schedules, and updates on local events. Lastly, if you're traveling with kids or have accessibility needs, the **Bordeaux-Lac Tourism Center** offers special resources, including family-friendly itineraries and details on accessible attractions. This center is especially helpful for those visiting the lake and surrounding leisure spots.

Make sure to download the **Bordeaux CityPass**, which includes access to public transport, discounts at over 20 museums, and a guided tour option. You can purchase it at any tourist center

Embassy and Consulate Information

While Bordeaux doesn't have as many embassies as Paris, key consular services are still available. The **British Consulate** is located at **353 Boulevard du Président Wilson**, open Monday to Friday for British nationals needing assistance with passport services, legal advice, or travel emergencies. For American tourists, the **U.S. Consular Agency** in Bordeaux at **34 Rue Charles Domercq** can help with emergency passport replacements, legal inquiries, or notary services. It's best to call ahead for appointments at **+33 5 56 51 66 65**.

Other English-speaking services are available through the **Australian Honorary Consulate** at **Rue Ferrère**. They offer limited services such as document notarization or providing emergency assistance. Make sure to keep these contacts handy for any travel emergencies.

Emergency Numbers and Local Authorities

France has a highly efficient emergency service system. The most important number to remember is **112**, which connects you to all emergency services, including police, fire, and medical aid. For direct police assistance, dial **17**, while **18** will connect you to the fire department.

For medical emergencies, call **15** to reach an ambulance service. Bordeaux has several hospitals, the most prominent being the **CHU Pellegrin** located at **Place Amélie Raba Léon**, which has an emergency department for tourists. Pharmacies are plentiful in Bordeaux, with many offering 24-hour services—look for the green cross signs indicating open ones. Pharmacies also provide advice on minor health concerns.

Travel insurance is highly recommended, as it will help you access private healthcare or cover any unforeseen medical costs during your stay.

Recommended Travel Agencies and Tour Operators

Bordeaux offers a wealth of travel agencies that can help you make the most of your visit. **Bordeaux Wine Trails** is highly recommended for wine enthusiasts, offering small group tours that explore Bordeaux's famous vineyards. They provide immersive experiences that include wine tastings and visits to prestigious châteaux.

For city tours, **Bordeaux Walking Tours** is a fantastic option for those interested in history and architecture. They offer themed walking tours, including explorations of Bordeaux's medieval past, its wine history, or specific areas like the Chartrons district.

For those looking for day trips, **Aquitaine Travel Tours** specializes in excursions to the Dordogne Valley, Arcachon Bay, and other nearby attractions. They offer both private and small group options with multilingual guides. All these agencies can be contacted online for booking and provide customizable itineraries to suit your preferences.

CONCLUSION

Thank you for choosing this guidebook as your companion on your journey through Bordeaux. It has been a privilege to share with you the rich history, beautiful landscapes, and hidden gems of this extraordinary region. From iconic vineyards to lesser-known wineries, from the bustling heart of Bordeaux to its tranquil countryside, this book has aimed to offer you insights, tips, and an unforgettable experience.

As you go on your adventures, I pray for safe travels and enriching experiences that fill your heart with joy and wonder. May the sights you see, the wine you taste, and the people you meet leave you with lasting memories and a deeper appreciation for this remarkable part of France.

May this guidebook have served you well, providing the information and resources you needed to make the most of your trip. May you find beauty in every corner of Bordeaux, and may your journey be as delightful and enriching as you hoped.

Safe travels, and may your experiences in Bordeaux be as wonderful as the land itself.

Bon voyage!

Bonus: Special Map of Vineyards with Tips for Off-the-Beaten-Path Wineries

1. Château Brethous (Cadillac)

Located in Cadillac, Château Brethous is a family-run vineyard with a focus on biodynamic and organic farming. Known for its Merlot, Malbec, and Viognier grapes, it's an ideal stop for eco-conscious travelers. The serene setting and commitment to sustainability make the wine-tasting experience here feel intimate and authentic.

Tip: Less than an hour from Bordeaux, book a private tour in advance for an immersive experience with the winemakers themselves.

2. Château de la Rivière (Fronsac)

Situated in the Fronsac appellation, Château de la Rivière offers incredible views of the Dordogne River. The hidden gem is known for its deep history and stunning underground cellars. A tour here not only covers their unique winemaking process but also includes a journey through centuries-old cellars carved into limestone.

Tip: Consider a sunset wine tasting here, which allows you to enjoy the vineyard's wines with the Dordogne River as a beautiful backdrop.

3. Château d'Armajan des Ormes (Sauternes)

This family-run vineyard in Sauternes is renowned for producing some of the finest sweet wines in Bordeaux. The brothers who run the estate offer intimate tours, explaining the detailed process of crafting Sauternes wines, and even include tastings of their best vintages.

Tip: Visit during the fall to witness the Sauternes harvest season, when the grapes reach their peak ripeness for dessert wine production.

4. Château Peybonhomme-Les-Tours (Blaye)

One of the oldest family-run estates in Bordeaux, Château Peybonhomme-Les-Tours is known for its biodynamic practices and organic wines. The estate produces exceptional Merlot and Cabernet blends and offers serene, personalized tastings.

Tip: Combine your visit with a bike tour through the scenic Blaye region, where you can explore other small vineyards and enjoy the countryside.

5. Château de Reignac (Entre-Deux-Mers)

This château combines historical charm with modern winemaking techniques. It offers unique tasting sessions in its glasshouse, which was designed by Gustave Eiffel. The scenic property and award-winning wines make this a must-visit for wine aficionados.

Tip: Schedule a tasting in the glasshouse for an exclusive experience and don't miss their special wine blending sessions.

6. Château La Croizille (Saint-Émilion)

Château La Croizille is a small but significant vineyard located on Saint-Émilion's elevated plateau. Known for its stunning views and focus on blending traditional and innovative winemaking techniques, this is an intimate, family-run vineyard experience.

Tip: Pair your wine tasting with a picnic on the vineyard's terrace. You'll be treated to sweeping views of the vines and surrounding countryside.

7. Château Coutet (Saint-Émilion)

Sitting on the highest hill in Saint-Émilion, Château Coutet boasts a unique terroir of sand, limestone, and clay. The historic vineyard is perfect for history buffs, offering cellar tours that reveal Roman artifacts and underground fortifications.

Tip: Don't miss their underground wine cellar, a hidden treasure that houses some of their best aging wines.

8. Château Lamothe Bergeron (Médoc)

This vineyard in the Médoc region offers a variety of experiences tailored to different levels of wine enthusiasts. Known for its structured Cabernet Sauvignon blends, the estate provides both cellar tours and immersive wine-tasting sessions in its picturesque setting.

Tip: Visit during the summer for their exclusive "gourmet" wine-tasting events that pair local cuisine with their signature wines.

9. Château Puyanché (Francs Côtes de Bordeaux)

Château Puyanché is a quaint, family-owned vineyard in one of Bordeaux's smallest appellations. Known for its rustic charm, the vineyard offers a peaceful setting and produces excellent Merlot and Cabernet Franc blends.

Tip: Combine your visit with nearby medieval villages like Saint-Émilion to make the most of your trip to this lesser-known part of Bordeaux.

10. Château de Ferrand (Saint-Émilion)

Château de Ferrand is a large Grand Cru Classé winery offering detailed tours of its extensive estate and cellars. The 17th-century château provides a more polished wine-tasting experience but still offers a personal touch with its small, well-curated events.

Tip: Opt for a masterclass in wine tasting to deepen your understanding of Saint-Émilion's terroir.

Navigating Between Vineyards

The best way to explore these off-the-beaten-path wineries is by car. Renting a car gives you the flexibility to explore multiple regions in a day. If you prefer not to drive, several local tour companies offer customized wine tours that focus on hidden gems. **Bordeaux with Élodie** and **Aquitaine Travel Tours** are highly recommended for private tours that take you off the typical tourist trails. Alternatively, cycling tours are popular in regions like Entre-Deux-Mers and Blaye, where the terrain is more forgiving.

Insider Tips

- **Book in advance:** Many of these boutique wineries offer private tours and tastings that require reservations.

- **Vineyard events:** Check the winery's calendar for events like picnics, live music, and themed wine tastings.

- **Travel light:** Some of these wineries are more remote and may have limited services, so pack essentials like water and snacks.

Make sure to contact the vineyards in advance to schedule tours, as many of these smaller wineries require reservations for tastings and private visits.

Made in United States
North Haven, CT
27 April 2025